MARION STROUD

It's Just You & Me, Lord

PRAYERS FOR A WOMAN'S LIFE

DISCOVERY HOUSE

PUBLISHERS®

Feeding the Soul with the Word of God

It's Just You and Me, Lord: Prayers for a Woman's Life
© 2012 by Marion Stroud
All rights reserved.

Discovery House is affiliated with RBC Ministries, Grand Rapids, Michigan.

Requests for permission to quote from this book should be directed to: Permissions Department, Discovery House Publishers, P.O. Box 3566, Grand Rapids, MI 49501, or contact us by e-mail at permissionsdept@dhp.org

Scriptures taken from the Holy Bible, New International Version®, NIV®. Copyright © 1973, 1978, 1984 by Biblica, Inc.™ Used by permission of Zondervan. All rights reserved worldwide. www.zondervan.com

Scripture quotations marked NLT are from the *Holy Bible,* New Living Translation, copyright © 1996, 2004. Used by permission of Tyndale House Publishers, Inc., Wheaton, Illinois 60189. All rights reserved.

Published in association with the Books & Such Literary Agency, Mary Keeley, 52 Mission Circle, Suite 122, PMB 170, Santa Rosa, CA 95409-5370. www.booksandsuch.biz

Interior design by Sherri L. Hoffman

Library of Congress Cataloging-in-Publication Data

Stroud, Marion.
    It's just you and me, Lord : prayers for a woman's life / Marion Stroud.
       p. cm.
    Includes bibliographical references.
    ISBN 978-1-57293-573-0
1. Christian women—Prayers and devotions. 2. Prayers. I. Title.
    BV4844.S766 2012
    242'.843--dc23

                          2012017721

Printed in the United States of America
First printing this edition in 2014

Contents

A WOMAN AND HER CHILDREN

A WOMAN AND HER FRIENDS

A WOMAN AT WORK

A WOMAN AND HER FAMILY OF FAITH

A WOMAN AND THE WIDER WORLD

A WOMAN GROWING OLDER

Introduction

One of my favorite ways of spending an evening is to share a meal with old friends. What we eat and drink is not particularly important—it's the conversation that matters. We look back and laugh about our youthful escapades. We talk about the issues that confront us now and wrestle with questions of faith and family. Nothing is off-limits. We challenge each other's presuppositions and get fresh glimpses of truth through the eyes of a trusted companion.

Prayer, at its best, is like sharing a meal with a loved and trusted friend. Jesus says, "Look! I stand at the door and knock. If you hear my voice and open the door, I will come in, and we will share a meal together as friends" (Revelation 3:20 NLT).

Some of the topics I have written about in these pages spring from my own experience, but many are rooted in the pain and challenges faced by others. In some cases the details of the situation have been changed to protect their privacy. But all these conversations with God spring from life as we experience it in the twenty-first century.

> Prayer is not an old woman's idle amusement. Properly understood and applied, it is the most potent instrument of action.
>
> 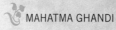 MAHATMA GHANDI

You may want to make my words your own, or simply use them as a prompt for your own communication with our loving heavenly Father. Whatever words you use, you can approach Him boldly, confident that as you honestly and openly share your joys, your pain, and your perplexity with Him, you will come away from the encounter changed and strengthened.

A WOMAN WITHIN

Oh, the comfort, the inexpressible comfort of feeling safe
with a person, having neither to weigh thoughts nor
measure words, but only to pour them all right out just as
they are, chaff and grain together, knowing that a faithful
hand will take and sift them, keep what is worth keeping,
and then with the breath of kindness blow the rest away.

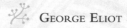 GEORGE ELIOT

God loves me unconditionally. And He will love me into perfection. With Him I can be absolutely open, sharing the best and worst of my life, my joys and my sorrows, because He knows about every detail already. Nothing I can say or do will affect our relationship for good or for evil. I am His beloved child who delights His heart. He is the always available, unshockable friend, the relentless lover, and the hiding place in which I can rest safely, whatever storms may rock my world.

Summer Suns Are Glowing

Arise, my darling, my beautiful one,
and come with me.
See! The winter is past;
the rains are over and gone.
Flowers appear on the earth;
the season of singing has come.

SONG OF SOLOMON 2:10–12

~

Summertime,
and the livin' is easy.
Fish are jumping,
and the cotton is high.

DUBOSE HEYWARD

The long dark days of winter are over, Lord,
and everything within me
wants to make the very best
of this bright time of year.
As I awaken to the song of birds,
cause me to add my song of praise
under my breath,
beneath the rattle
of the commuter train,
or ringing round the bathroom as I shower.

Thank you for opportunities to walk and talk with you
while, as the old song puts it,[1]
the dew is still on the roses,
and the earth
smells fresh and sweet.
Thank you for ripening fruit on trees,
fields of standing corn,
and farmers' markets
overflowing
with fruit and vegetables of every hue.

Thank you for opportunities
to stop and stare, dear Lord.
For some there will be no vacations
in peaceful countryside or by the sea.
But all of us can pause for
    one brief moment
to smell a rose,
to watch a spider spin its
    web,
or simply be aware
of all the little things

that bring your joy into
the present moment.

Thank you for the fun of
outdoor eating.

The clink of ice in glass and fragrant smoke
from barbecue or campfire embers.
Help us to grasp the opportunity
to open up our hearts and home

You care for the land and water it . . .
You crown the year with your bounty,
    and your carts overflow with
        abundance . . .
The meadows are covered with flocks
    and the valleys are mantled with
        grain;
    they shout for joy
    and sing.

PSALM 65:9–13

to old and young,
inviting friend and stranger
to share in our enjoyment.

And as the evening darkens,
calm our hearts
to see the glory of the sunset,
and the bright twinkle of the stars
against the velvet darkness of the sky,
as treasures from your hand,
filling us
with reverence for the things you have made,
and thankfulness
for summertime.

Will the Real Me Please Stand?

I searched everywhere, determined to find wisdom and to understand the reason for things.

ECCLESIASTES 7:25 NLT

~

She wants to live for once. But doesn't know quite what that means. Wonders if she's ever done it. If she ever will.

ALICE WALKER

~

"I have come that they may have life, and have it to the full."

JOHN 10:10

"I'm sorry, I don't know your name," she said.
"I always think of you as David's mother."
"Are you the dentist's wife?" the nurse inquired, advancing on me,
ready to take a sample of my blood.
"I think he's wonderful!"

"I was expecting a real 'earth-mother' type
when I was told you had so many children,"

she murmured cheerfully,
waiting for a chance to introduce me
to the noisy group
of coffee-drinking women,
"but actually, you look quite elegant!"

Dear Lord, these people know me
only through my association
with someone else.
And really, I can't blame them.
For there are days when I stop and wonder
who this woman really is,
whom I see daily in the mirror.
I am amazed at times
to think that she is me.

I'm usually too busy, Lord,
to think about
these challenging life questions.
But today,
when I have been reminded
that you intend your children
to have life in all its fullness,
I really need to ask you what you meant,
when you voiced such an all-encompassing remark
to your disciples.

I have to say,
if you were meaning "lots to do,"
then I've received your gift already.
My days are packed
and stretch into the night,
while I whirl around

cooking, cleaning, checking details,
and doing all the rest that must be done
to keep a family headed
in the right direction.

And yet somehow I can't believe
that this is all my life is meant to be about.
If you have made me
unique and special,
as your Word tells me that you have,
numbering my days,
counting every hair and catching every tear,
blessing me with gifts,
and giving me a purpose to fulfill
in your economy,
then surely there is more to life
than what I do for
    other people.
Please help me, Lord.

Enable me to find that
    sacred space
where I can meet
    with you.
Then you can gently
    take apart
the many layered
    Russian doll
that often seems to represent my life,
and show me who the "real me" is,
so that I can embrace
all that I am, and all you have for me
with joy and thankfulness.

> At any moment an unsatisfying life may become once more a grand adventure, if we will surrender it to God. The adventure of faith is exciting, difficult and exacting, but full of new discoveries, fresh turns and sudden surprises.
>
> PAUL TOURNIER

A Different Kind of Fast

*"Is not this the kind of fasting I have chosen: to loose
the chains of injustice . . . to set the oppressed free
and break every yolk? Is it not to share your food with
the hungry and to provide the poor wanderer with
shelter—when you see the naked, to clothe him, and
not to turn away from your own flesh and blood?"*

ISAIAH 58:6–7

You know, dear Lord,
I've always struggled with the thought of fasting.
Of going without food or drink
or other fleshly things
that make life easy,
in order to do . . . what?
Draw near to you or hear your voice
more clearly?

You know that I have tried it, Lord,
without a great deal of success.
And yet I really want to change
and get to know you better.
So this year, will you be with me
as I try out
a different kind of fast?

I know I have a weakness, Lord,
for being quick to notice
when family or friends
may fail to measure up
to what I arrogantly judge
to be desirable behavior,
while I give little thought
to the many ways in which I fall short.

Forgive me, Lord, and help me as I choose this day
to fast from criticism and feast on praise.

You've given me so much, dear Lord,
and I am richly blessed,
and yet so prone
to sink into the mire of pitying myself
and casting envious looks at other people—
not noticing their pain
or all the challenges they face,
but seeing only that they seem to have
the little things I lack.

Forgive me, Lord, and help me as I choose this day
to fast from pitying myself and feast on joy.

I'm well aware that I am not
a morning person.
And there are times first thing
when I'm not very nice
to be around.
My grumpiness can be a form of self-indulgence,
when I allow myself to treat my family
with less respect
than I will later offer to the folks at work.

Forgive me, Lord, and help me as I choose this day
to fast from ill temper and feast on peace.

You know that there are times
when I get really scared,
allowing fearful thoughts
to fill my mind
about the future or the ones I love.
And I forget that you have promised
that you will never leave me
to face the fire or floods
of difficulty or loss alone.

Forgive me, Lord, and help me as I choose this day
to fast from fear and feast on faith in you.

Although it's good
to do the best we can, Lord,
I know that I am easily trapped
by the desire of wanting everything
to be completely flawless,
rejecting offers
of less-than-expert help
and then complaining
that everything is left to me.

Only you are perfect, Lord,
and you accept us as we are.

Forgive me, Lord, and help me as I choose this day
to fast from trying to be perfect
and feast on knowing that you will receive with joy
the best that I can do for now.

Rest

"Remember to observe the Sabbath day by keeping it holy. You have six days each week for your ordinary work, but the seventh day is a Sabbath day of rest dedicated to the Lord your God."

EXODUS 20:8–10 NLT

~

When was the last time you asked forgiveness for not resting?

LYNN PENSON

~

When we spend a day resting, focused only on loving God and loving others, we experience the presence of Jesus in simple things. We experience peace, the sacredness of the ordinary. What if we had a day focused . . . on true connectedness, a day when we unplug our electronics but plug in to others? . . . To spend time, as Jesus did, and allow them to change us and us to change them.

KERI WYATT KENT

I'd never thought of it before, Lord.
So when the preacher asked us
if we had ever sought forgiveness
for regularly ignoring your command
to rest for one day out of seven,
I must confess that I was shocked.

Can it really be that vital
to lay aside the daily chores,
as much as we are able,
so that we rest our minds and bodies,
but most of all spend time,
like Mary,
sitting at your feet?

I guess it must be so, because we find it
among those rules for life
that we have called the Ten Commandments.
Rest is listed just below the prohibition
of other gods or idols
and the command
to treat
your name with reverence.
It seems that it's considered even more important
than what we class as major sins,
like failing
to show our parents due respect,
or giving way to murder or adultery,
theft and lying,
or coveting
the things and the relationships belonging to another.

But in the modern world it seems
that we've become addicted
to busyness.
It makes us feel important, needed,
and better
than other people.

And then we start to see our overloaded lives
as a false measure

of how much we are valued
instead of finding our security
in your acceptance of us
just as we are.

The trouble is, dear Lord,
that our lifestyles today
are so far removed from life in Bible times
that it just seems impossible
to realistically compare the two.
So I need you to teach me
how I might begin to keep the Sabbath.

Here I am, Lord, truly wanting
to learn what I must do
in order to receive your gift of rest.
Help me to slow down
and pay attention to your voice.
To find a rhythm to my life,
as I look back, enjoying
the achievements of the week that's past,
before I rush ahead
into the next phase of activity.

Give me, dear Lord,
a fresh appreciation of the natural world
and help me learn to play again.
Replenish
the wells of my creativity,
and please reset my clamoring priorities
so that I stay aligned with you
as you reveal your pattern for my life.

What's in a Name?

The name of God matters as it defines him and our names matter too because they define us in many ways. What others call us matters. It matters because in our woundedness we assimilate those names within ourselves. "Sticks and stones . . . but names will never hurt me" is a lie. When, as pre-adolescents, we were labeled "different" or "weird" some of us internalized a life-long stigma in our own minds . . . When we were constantly picked last on the playground, we were named "unchosen." When we were abandoned by a parent, we were named "unworthy." When we were abused, we were named "worthless."

JOHN MARK HICKS

~

To him who overcomes I will give . . . a white stone with a new name written on it, known only to him who receives it.

REVELATION 2:17

The newest member of our family, Lord,
is to be called a name
that I can neither spell nor easily pronounce.
But I suppose it's really not surprising,
when sports stars and celebrities
seem to delight to name their infants
after the place in which they were conceived,
or to reflect

their parents' favorite starring role
on stage or screen,
that ordinary folk are tempted to abandon
traditional names.
And even those who favor names found in the Bible
dig out the most obscure ones they can find.

Our names are funny things, Lord.
We may dislike the
   name our parents
     chose for us
or be quite happy
   with it,
but loved or hated
we rarely change it,
because so often that
   given name
defines us in some
   peculiar way.

> You will be called by a new name
> that the mouth of the Lord will bestow . . .
> No longer will they call you Deserted,
> or name your land Desolate.
> But you will be called Hephzibah,
> and your land Beulah;
> for the Lord will take delight in you,
> and your land will be married . . .
> As a bridegroom rejoices over his bride,
> so will your God rejoice over you.
>
> ISAIAH 62:2–5

Though we may not
   want to change
our public name, Lord,
there is so often
a need for ruthlessly removing
the labels others put on us,
or else the names we give ourselves.

These names are rarely kind or complimentary,
and we can quietly batter
our hearts and spirits
by listening to other people

or ourselves,
say words like *lazy, stupid, fearful,*
total failure,
a person whom no one could really love,
and who is destined
to walk through life uncared for and *alone.*

One thing that I have noticed about you, Lord,
is that if you should change a person's name,
it's usually because
you have done something in their lives
that indicates that they are now
a new and different person.

So Lord, when we become aware
that you have changed us from the inside out,
help us to leave those painful labels in the past
and to embrace the new name
that you have offered in your Word.

Please firstly change our hearts.
Then give us "godly spectacles" with which to view ourselves
and ears to hear your loving whispers:
"You are my beloved;
on you my favor rests.
I delight in you and rejoice over you
with singing."

Hide-and-Seek

Jonah ran away from the Lord and headed for Tarshish.
He went down to Joppa, where he found a ship bound
for that port. After paying the fare, he went aboard
and sailed for Tarshish to flee from the Lord.

JONAH 1:3

~

I fled Him, down the nights and down the days;
I fled Him, down the arches of the years;
I fled Him, down the labyrinthine ways
Of my own mind; and in the mist of tears
I hid from Him, and under running laughter . . .
From those strong Feet that followed, followed after.
But with unhurrying chase,
And unperturbèd pace,
Deliberate speed, majestic instancy,
They beat—and a Voice beat
More instant than the Feet—
"All things betray thee, who betrayest Me."

FRANCIS THOMPSON, "THE HOUND OF HEAVEN"

Have you got a minute, Lord?
I know that it has been a long, long while
since you and I
have had a conversation.

In fact I come here now
with stomach churning,
uncertain
whether I'll be welcome.
Why would you want to hear from someone
who has been playing
hide-and-seek with you for
    many years?

Strangely enough,
hide-and-seek is not a game
I'm very keen on.
For even as a child
I found that hiding in the
    barn
while others hunted for me
scared me so much
that I was often tempted
to jump out and shout
"I'm here!"
just to end the terror.

> The Hound of Heaven has been
> pursuing us through the years, baying
> ever on our track. It was we who
> needed to give assent to his presence,
> not he who had to be attracted and
> come to us. And when he enters in
> and sups with us and we with him,
> what unspeakable joy! At last we are
> home.
>
> THOMAS KELLY [1893–1941]

And then there was that day
when friends got tired of searching
and went away to play another game,
leaving me immobile in the dusty darkness,
silent and afraid.
I was torn
between a passionate desire
to be the winner
and a longing
for someone, anyone, to find me.
That is how it's been for us, Lord.

I wanted my own way,
thought walking in your paths would be restrictive,
and insisted I knew best,
though sometimes I was secretly afraid
that if I pushed you to the limit,
you too would walk away
and leave me to my own devices.

So have you, Lord?
Have you tired of waiting
and simply looked elsewhere
for someone else?
Someone who's less stubborn and resistant
to walking in your paths
than I have been?

I know, Lord, that you told the story of a prodigal
who lived a life of partying,
making friends with dubious morals,
with whom no mother
would want to see her child
    keep company.
But when he finally got tired
of eating pig food,
and turned his face to home,
he found a joyful welcome
with ring and robe and fatted
    calf,
however differently
his brother saw the situation.
But is it true for living people, Lord?
Am I still welcome in your church,
as part of your forever family?

> "Here I am! I stand at the door and knock. If anyone hears my voice and opens the door, I will come in and eat with him, and he with me."
>
> REVELATION 3:20

And do the haunting lyrics
of that song I heard
whilst wakeful in the early hours—
"I am not forgotten, I am not forgotten,
I am not forgotten,
for Jesus knows my name"—
apply to someone
who has been as far away as me?

Because I need to tell you, Lord,
that if they do apply,
there's someone waiting
who's tired of hiding,
who wants to shout,
"I'm here!
Please find me
and take me back to where I can
belong again forever
in what used to be my home."

> The Lord is compassionate and merciful,
> slow to get angry and filled with unfailing love.
> He will not constantly accuse us,
> nor remain angry forever . . .
> He does not deal harshly with us, as we deserve.
> For his unfailing love toward those who fear him
> is as great as the height of the heavens above the earth.
> He has removed our sins as far from us
> as the east is from the west.
>
> PSALM 103:8–12 NLT

Free Indeed

*"Forgive us our sins, as we have
forgiven those who sin against us."*
MATTHEW 6:12 NLT

~

*Then Peter came to Jesus and asked, "Lord how
many times shall I forgive my brother when he sins
against me? Up to seven times?" Jesus answered,
"I tell you, not seven times, but seventy-seven times."*
MATTHEW 18:21–22

~

*To forgive is to set the prisoner free, and then
discover that the prisoner was you.*
LEWIS B. SMEDES

~

"If the Son sets you free, you will be free indeed."
JOHN 8:36

Dear Lord, I need to talk to you
about forgiveness.
Your Word is plain enough about the subject—
we must forgive.
But if the person who has sinned against me

appears to have no notion
of the pain that he has caused,
and has not shown the slightest inclination
to take responsibility for his share of blame
or to apologize
for his part in the breach between us,
what then?

I thought I had forgiven him.
I really did.
But if our conversation takes us near the area of life
in which I feel that I've been cheated,
wronged, shortchanged, and deeply hurt,
the anger and the bitterness rise up again
until I want to scream and shout,
"See what you did to me!
I need to hear you say, 'I'm sorry.'"

But it just doesn't happen, Lord,
and I am left with that old
    wound
ripped open once again.
I feel just like that sheep I saw
caught in the brambles.
Every time she struggled to get
    free,
she seemed to be more firmly
    held,
'til finally she was unable
to move at all.

I'm increasingly convinced that many life-threatening illnesses have their roots in bitterness and unforgiveness, so that the individual, who clings to her grievance, refusing to forgive unless the other person also recognizes his fault, puts her very life in danger.

A HOSPITAL CHAPLAIN

Please help me, Lord.
I feel so like that sheep today.
Immobilized by anger and frustration,
I need a shepherd who can cut me free,
apply a loving touch to wounded flesh,
and bring me home upon his shoulders.

Help me accept that just as I'm forgiven,
so you extend that grace to
    all who hurt me.
Enable me to give my pain
    to you
and lay this torn relationship
    before your cross,
remembering your words on
    Calvary:
"Father, forgive them,
for they do not know what
    they are doing."

You will know that forgiveness has begun when you recall those who hurt you and feel the power to wish them well.

LEWIS B. SMEDES

How Big Is Your God?

*A furious squall came up, and the waves broke over the boat, so
that it was nearly swamped. Jesus was in the stern, sleeping . . .
The disciples woke him and said to him, "Teacher, don't you care
if we drown?" He got up, rebuked the wind and said to the waves,
"Quiet! Be still!" Then the wind died down and it was completely
calm. He said to his disciples, "Why are you so afraid? Do you
still have no faith?" They were terrified and asked each other,
"Who is this? Even the wind and the waves obey him!"*

MARK 4:37–41

~

*God is good all the time;
all the time, God is good.*

TRADITIONAL SAYING

I'd heard it all before, Lord,
stories of life and love and loss
from one who's served you far away.
Living without clean water gushing from the tap,
electric power,
and all the other things that we assume
we need to function normally.
Stirring tales,
but so outside my everyday experience
that they seem hardly credible.

Questions came from every corner of the room.
How do you cope when . . .
Survive if . . .
Provide for the needs of . . .
Bear it when your children . . .
And with a smile,
to every query she replied,
"I've learned trust the Lord."

Can that be true, Lord?
Really?
Is it possible for anyone
to learn to lean upon you so completely?
Does she never have
dark hours of tossing through the night,
and then waking
heavyhearted,
weighed down with anxious thoughts?

Maybe it's easier
for those you call to serve you,
as we say,
"full-time."
They're probably a race apart,
equipped with special faith
for special circumstances.
But we were not allowed to hide behind
such thoughts as these.

Before the smell of coffee and a tempting plate of snacks
wafted us back into the safe
and the familiar,

her challenge,
tossed across the room,
silenced the gentle swell of chatter at a stroke.
"And you—
who do you really trust?"

Dear Lord, although I am ashamed
to put it into words,
I have to say it,
for you know anyway,
that I instinctively responded,
"I trust myself."

You know how I grew up, Lord.
Believing that I was responsible
to bring about
the kind of life I wanted,
and that if I did not protect,
initiate, and organize,
no one else would do it for me.

So I'm a planner,
a list maker.
One who loves control and
    order,
seeing this approach to be the
    only way
to keep things safe within my
    grasp.
And when I fret about the future,
I search for ways to rectify the situation
rather than bother you with my concerns.

> You, Lord, give perfect peace
> to those who keep their
> purpose firm and put their
> trust in You.
>
> ISAIAH 26:3,
> *Good News Translation*

Please help me, Lord.
Enlarge my vision;
expand my understanding.
Make it real to me that you are truly
all knowing, all powerful, always there.

If you can keep a tally of my hairs,
fallen sparrows,
and wayside flowers,
have storms and even death itself obey you,
then surely you have power enough
for every situation.

Wholehearted

He has showed you, O man, what is good. And
what does the Lord require of you? To act justly and
to love mercy and to walk humbly with your God.

MICAH 6:8

~

Give me an undivided heart,
that I may fear your name.

PSALM 86:11

~

"They will be my people, and I will be their God.
I will give them singleness of heart and action, so
that they will always fear me for their own good."

JEREMIAH 32:38–39

Dear Lord, I've always thought that it was good
to see both sides
of any situation.
To pause and think about the various advantages
of this way and of that.
But when it comes to making a decision,
it is so very hard to know
if it is your voice that I'm hearing,

or whether it's my own desires
that rattle round inside my head.

It's even worse when action
    must be taken.
You know I often turn into a
    block of ice,
incapable, it seems,
of doing what I know needs
    to be done.
Sometimes it doesn't matter
if I decide to leave my shopping for another day
or let dust bunnies decorate my shelves
a little longer.

But when I knowingly neglect that lump,
"forget" that difficult appointment,
put off the phone call,
withhold the money that I know that I should give,
avoid that pressing piece of work
until the need to get it done
means midnight oil is burnt
(threatening my job as well as
    my well-being),
then, Lord, I need what only
    you can give:
an undivided heart.

Please help me, Lord.
Retrain my focus.
Be, Lord, not simply of my heart
but of my actions and desires.

> Teach me your way, O Lord,
> and I will walk in your truth.
>
> PSALM 86:11

> Yesterday is a cancelled cheque.
> Tomorrow is a promissory note.
> Today is the only cash you have,
> so spend it wisely.
>
> KIM LYONS

Teach me to listen to your voice,
to recognize the wind-words of your Spirit.
Give me the thing I need so much,
the treasure that your Word has promised:
an undivided heart.

The really happy people are those
who have broken the chains of
procrastination, those who find
satisfaction in doing the job at hand.
They're full of eagerness, zest,
productivity. You can be, too.

NORMAN VINCENT PEALE

All Change . . .

"I am the Lord, and I do not change."

MALACHI 3:6 NLT

~

*To live is to change, and to be perfect
is to have changed often.*

CARDINAL NEWMAN

~

*Change is one of the few things in life that is certain,
since change and growth are two sides of the same coin.
Every period of change, whether it is from childhood to
adult life, singleness to marriage, middle life to old age
requires some degree of giving up and letting go. So growth
can either be a painful or a rewarding experience. It all
depends whether we fight it or accept it. Remember,
hands which are grimly clutching on to the past, are
totally unable to grasp hold of the present or future.*

SAINT FRANCIS OF ASSISI

Dear Lord, you know that I have always felt
uncomfortable with change.
And for the last twelve months it seems
as if my life has been

tipped out, tossed around,
and shaken up in all directions.

A year ago our daughter left for college
joyful, so ready with her loving hugs,
tossing kisses, waving us good-bye,
her car loaded with, it seemed,
the entire contents of her bedroom.
Then before we'd had a chance to settle down,
adjust to free use of the phone
and access to the bathroom,
our son and all his family
moved out of state.

Although I know they had to seize this opportunity
for what they think will be a better job,
more pay and prospects,
less pressure and more family time,
you know how much we miss them.

Now, Lord, our neighbors,
who've shared our lives for many years,
are seriously considering
purchasing a house
more suitable for their advancing age.
Disaster!
Who will I go to when my husband is abroad,
technology won't work,
my jam won't set, or black fly overcomes the roses?
They know just what to do
in areas that were excluded
from my expensive education.

Frankly, I am scared, dear Lord,
and some days really wonder how I'll manage
without these dear, familiar people close at hand.
It's at those times
I so badly need to hear your voice
reminding me
that every day is a love gift from you
to be savored, relished,
and received with thankfulness,
and your intention is for me
to take into the future
the best of every stage
    experienced so far.

Thank you
that while so many things are
    changing
that cannot be avoided,
got around, denied,
but simply must be taken
one step at a time,
there is no pathway that I'll have to tread
without your company.

Thank you too that
in these varied scenes of life,
one thing is certain—
you are immovable,
unshakeable,
unchangeable,
and unquestionably the same, yesterday, today, and forever.

> Everyone thinks of changing
> the world, but no one thinks of
> changing himself.
>
> LEO TOLSTOY

Dreams and Visions

[Jacob] had a dream in which he saw a stairway resting on the earth, with its top reaching to heaven, and the angels of God were ascending and descending on it. There above it stood the Lord, and he said: ". . . I am with you and will watch over you wherever you go, and I will bring you back to this land. I will not leave you until I have done what I have promised you." When Jacob awoke from his sleep, he thought, "Surely the Lord is in this place, and I was not aware of it."

GENESIS 28:12–16

~

I will lie down and sleep in peace,
for you alone, O Lord, make me dwell in safety.

PSALM 4:8

~

Those who dream by night in the dusty recesses of their minds wake in the day to find that all was vanity; but the dreamers of the day are dangerous men, for they may act their dream with open eyes, and make it possible.

T. E. LAWRENCE

Dear Lord, I really need to talk to you
about my dreams.
By that I don't mean idle thoughts that fill my mind

when I have nothing else to do,
or things I long to do for you
someday, maybe,
but rather images that fill my mind when I'm asleep.

The experts tell us, Lord, that we all dream
but that few of us remember
when morning comes.
And that is true of me
    sometimes.
But far more often,
my sleep is full
of dreams of rush and hurry
that leave me more exhausted
    when I wake
than when I went to bed.

> Every evening I turn my worries
> over to God. He's going to be
> up all night anyway.
>
> MARY C. CROWLEY

I know that in the Bible
you often spoke to men and women
while they slept.
Jacob saw a ladder up to heaven,
kings and leaders
were made to face the challenge of their sin,
Joseph and the wise men were steered to safety,
and Paul was given his next mission
in a dream.

So if you have important things to say to me
while I'm asleep,
then I am ready.
For I've already learned
that when I have those dreams of panic,

trains that I can't catch,
packing forgotten or not done,
keys or children lost,
that I am overloaded in the day.

And when I dream of struggling up a tower or scaffold,
which I can only mount if I accept
the help of others,
the meaning is quite obvious,
and I do thank you for the insights
that you have given me in
this way.

Lord, I wouldn't want to
miss
your message of direction.
If I wake up as Samuel did
with your voice ringing in
my ear,
then, Lord, I want to say,
"Please speak, for I am listening."

But Lord, apart from that,
I am so very, very tired,
and I would really love to have
just a few nights,
occasionally,
of peaceful, dreamless sleep!

From all ill dreams defend our eyes,
from nightly fears and fantasies;
tread under foot our ghostly foe,
that no pollution we may know.

ANCIENT COMPLINE HYMN

Just an Ordinary Day

Make every day a cathedral, giving glory to God.

ANN VOSKAMP

~

Shout for joy to the Lord, all the earth.
Worship the Lord with gladness;
come before him with joyful songs . . .
Enter his gates with thanksgiving
and his courts with praise;
give thanks to him and praise his name.

PSALM 100:1–4

Today was just an ordinary day.
Routine, mundane, full of chores,
small decisions,
minor crises.
And yet, Lord, if I pause to think,
it has been full of touches of your love.

Thank you for my family.
We breakfasted together
and no one
fought for possession of the newspaper,
spilled the coffee, burned the toast,
tripped over the dog,

or had their mobile phone taken away
for texting at the table!

Thank you that the beginning of this day
was not made harder by reluctant risers,
fear of a test
or worries about a feuding friend.
Thank you for cheerful conversation,
help given unasked,
and a kiss in passing from a son,
who long since thought himself too old
for such an obvious offering of affection.

Thank you, God, that you've entrusted
this motley group of people
whom we call family,
to our care.
And thank you for a
    husband
who shares the joys
    and sorrows
with unruffled calm
and not a little
    humor.
So though we'll still
    experience
unplanned expenses
and health concerns,
we can rejoice in
    days like this,
enlivened by your touch
and filled with love and laughter.

The Greek translation of *Eucharisteo* means to give thanks. It's what Jesus did at the last supper, at the end of his earthly life, and what I committed to do with all of my life. To take up each day and give thanks for it, to take each moment and savor it, a morsel from His hand, and find sustenance and God in it.

ANN VOSKAMP

Help me appreciate
the "ordinary" days more often,
pausing more readily to stand and stare
and to enjoy the little things
that I so often stumble past
when I have people to see,
places to go.
Help me to remember how it was today
when storms blow up again,
still offering you my "Eucharisteo"—
my song of gratitude and joy.

Gratitude is not about "looking at the bright side" or denying the realities of life. Gratitude goes much deeper than that. It's about learning from a situation, taking the good to help deal with other challenges in the future. It's about finding out that you have more power over your life than you previously imagined. You can stop being a victim of your circumstances and reach out to the joy in living. If you open your heart to the good in your life, gratitude becomes as much a part of your life as breathing.

JOAN BUCHMAN

Pierced Ears

*If you buy a Hebrew servant, he is to serve you for six years.
But in the seventh year, he shall go free, without paying
anything . . . But if the servant declares, "I love my master
. . . and do not want to go free," then his master must take him
before the judges. He shall take him to the . . . doorpost and
pierce his ear with an awl. Then he will be his servant for life.*

EXODUS 21:2–6

~

*This letter is from Paul, a slave of Christ Jesus, chosen by
God to be an apostle and sent out to preach his Good News.*

ROMANS 1:1 NLT

As I walked through the mall today, dear Lord,
I counted just how many teenagers
had body piercings
of one kind or another.
I don't think I saw one without an earring,
and many others
had both nose and eyebrows pierced.

What do they see in it, dear Lord?
It must be very painful,
with not a little risk of serious infection.
Maybe they just want to be

like others of their age,
deeming it to well worth the pain
if in this way they're "in the current style."

At one time piercing was
a symbol of rebellion, Lord.
A longing to be different.
And even now
parents may shudder when the topic's aired
around their family dinner table,
for Christians have so many different views
about this rather controversial issue.

But as I think of simple earrings, Lord,
I wonder if I'd be so keen to wear them
if I'd been told that pierced ears are essential
to symbolize
that I'm a Christian.
Would I be happy to go through the pain
and have my faith made visible
for all to see?
Especially if it was clearly understood by all who saw it
that, like the slaves I read of in your Word,
an ear pierced by the master meant
that I had willingly surrendered
my freedom and my rights,
and was now his willing slave for life.

You know, Lord, in these days
that we would call "enlightened,"
we rightly value
equality for all.

And we would guard those hard-won freedoms
the law refers to as our "human rights"
with all our hearts.
It makes the very notion
of being a bond slave
of anyone
both countercultural and alien.

And yet, dear Lord,
you suffered body piercings
to an unspeakable degree.
There was a day in history when you allowed
the soldiers of an occupying power
to drive nails through your hands and feet,
and then to hoist you up upon a cross,
where you laid down your life in order to ensure
that I can be forgiven.

So when your servant Paul suggests
that it is eminently reasonable
to offer up our bodies
as willing sacrifices
in view of all that you have done for us,
dare I demur?
Please help me, Lord.
For you know just how quickly
I tend to rise up from the altar
in order
to go my own sweet way,
forgetting what I signed up for
when I committed
myself to you,
for time and for eternity.

Cultivating My Inner Garden

The crops are in, the summer is over,
but for us nothing's changed.
We're still waiting to be rescued.

JEREMIAH 8:20, THE MESSAGE

~

Do not stare at me because . . . I am darkened by the
sun. My mother's sons . . . made me take care of the
vineyards; my own vineyard I have neglected.

SONG OF SOLOMON 1:6

Lord, you know I always have high hopes of summer.
I dream of sun-drenched relaxation,
carefree days fun-packed and fruitful.
I tell myself that I will have time to
tackle jobs that normally get shelved,
rise and pray when I am woken by the light—
instead of snuggling down beneath the sheets—
and exercise much more
to lose the weight that has been hidden
beneath my winter clothes.

Today in church we celebrated
another season full of food

and your material provision for winter months to come,
but once again, dear Lord, I realize
the summer's ended
without the personal harvest I had hoped for.
And as the new season begins,
am I to see my hopes of change and fruitfulness
buried beneath the fallen leaves of busyness?
Am I just sitting here,
hoping for someone else to do for me
what only I can do?
Am I, like those in Jeremiah's day, still "waiting to be
    rescued"?

Thank you for the reminder in the service, Lord,
that just as I have spent last week
preparing house and garden for the winter months ahead,
so I can "autumn clean" my inner life
in order to prepare for future productivity.
Those lovely shrubs I planted years ago
are now so large that they are threatening
to choke out other plants,
and I have had to cut them back.
Please show me if there are things in my life
that once were right and beautiful,
but now need pruning,
or even to be pulled out altogether,
in order to make room for new directions in my life.

I have enjoyed the fruit and vegetables I planted,
but now the plants' productivity is at an end.
The ground in which they've grown is best turned over,
and then left fallow for a season

before I plant again.
In the same way, dear Lord,
help me to see just where I need to rest.
Or maybe I need to learn new skills.
Should I be planting bulbs that at the moment
do not appear to be alive at all,
but that, I trust,
given the right conditions,
will flower in spring and brighten all our lives?

Then finally, dear Lord, there are some jobs
that I don't have the skill or expertise
to tackle on my own.
Help me to come to you for changes
that only you can bring about.
And if I need humility in order to ask others
to listen and support me,
then help me to do that,
because I really want my inner garden to produce
the lovely fruit that you've designed it for.

A Woman and Marriage

Marriage is an art, and just like any other creative process,
it needs both active thought and effort.
We have to learn to share on many different levels.
We have to practice talking from the heart,
while understanding attitudes and body language, as well
*   as words.*
Giving generously and receiving graciously are talents that
*   are available to anyone to learn.*
But all these skills must be developed,
if the marriage picture that we want to paint is to be
*   anything approaching*
the masterpiece that God intended.

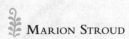 MARION STROUD

Becoming One

To become "one flesh" means two people become completely one, in body, soul, and spirit and yet remain two different persons. This is the innermost mystery of marriage.

WALTER TROBISCH

~

Marriage is a dynamic process of discovery,
a journey, not an arrival.
Marriage is starting to love,
over and over again.
It is a life's work.
In marriage, being the right person is
as important as finding the right person.

ANONYMOUS

At first I had no problem with this biblical idea, Lord,
that marriage should be such a fusion of our lives
that we are like one person.
But now that I have really thought about it,
I have to ask myself—and you,
"How can this work?"

Is it really possible
to be so joined
in heart and in emotion

with someone else,
that we can be like two sides of a coin,
while still retaining
our own identities?
And is this something that occurred
when we exchanged our rings?
Or does it have to be a process
that will take
a lifetime to complete?

The physical expression of our love
is the most obvious example
of those brief moments
when we can say we are "one flesh."
And that can bring great joy and satisfaction.
But for the most part, Lord,
we're just two people,
who love each other certainly,
but are so different.

You know how much
our interests and our natural talents vary.
We have a different outlook
on so many things.
Even in the spiritual dimension
he takes a practical approach
to the outworking of his faith,
while I am much more prone to question
and to explore theology from every angle.

So if we're destined to be "one," dear Lord,
which "one" will get the upper hand

and govern who we are?
I certainly don't want to fade out as a person,
lose sight of who I am,
and cease to be the "me" he fell in love with.
That makes it sound more like a takeover
than what I've always thought of
as an equal partnership.

Lord, help us please.
I really have to grit my teeth sometimes
in order not to argue back
when he assumes we'll always go his way
just like his father did before him.
And there are days when I take greater pleasure
in scoring points and proving
that I am right—
and thus maintaining what I perceive to be
that all-important,
superior position in our relationship—
than letting go of issues
that lack significance in the eternal scheme of things
in order to enjoy what we can agree on.

Please help security to grow, dear Lord,
so that within the certainty
and the protection
of one another's love and understanding,
we can enjoy a special kind of freedom.
The freedom to live out our full potential
in all the many ways
that we could never do alone.

Then maybe marriage will become
more like a merger.
A fusion of our lives
so that one person's weaknesses
are covered by the other person's strengths.
An "adding to" rather than "detracting from"
for both of us.
Instead of cramping and confining us,
perhaps this oneness is intended to produce
a joyful new dimension to our lives.

The Gift of Words

*It is impossible to over-emphasize the immense
need men have to be really listened to, to be taken
seriously, to be understood . . . No one can develop
freely in this world and find a full life without
feeling understood by at least one person.*

PAUL TOURNIER

~

*Pleasant words are a honeycomb,
sweet to the soul and healing to the bones.*

PROVERBS 16:24

Thank you, God, for teaching us
to talk to one another.
Thank you for the gift of words.
Thank you that you have given us each other
with whom to share our hopes, our fears,
our problems, and our plans.

Thank you
that as we've grown in confidence,
we've proved that there need be no fear in love,
and so we can be absolutely honest,
totally ourselves,
without the risk of ridicule or rejection.

Thank you for teaching us to listen.
To listen with our hearts
as well as with our ears.
To sense the needs that may remain unspoken
beneath the stumbling efforts to explain
the inexplicable.

Thank you that when there are no words
to meet the situation,
then love can be a silent song.
A touch that says, "I'm in this situation with you."
A smile that reassures "you're doing fine."

Thank you
that we have learned the need for patience.
The discipline to talk things through
until I'm satisfied.
Even when we're more than likely
to choose to put his first solution
into practice,
after all our words!

> God gave us two ears but only one mouth . . . perhaps a divine indication that we should listen twice as much as we talk.
>
> JOHN POWELL

Thank you
that I have learned to be a little
    more concise,
and he has learned
to keep on listening,
and to say ten words instead of two
until I see the situation clearly
and my heart feels understood.

Thank you, God, for teaching us to talk to one another.
Thank you for the gift of words.

The Walled Garden

You are my private garden, my treasure, my bride,
a secluded spring, a hidden fountain.

SONG OF SONGS 4:12 NLT

~

Your marriage should have within it a secret and protected
place, open to you alone. Imagine it to be a walled garden,
entered by a door to which you only hold the key. Within
this garden you will cease to be a mother, father, employee,
homemaker, or any of the other roles that you fulfill in daily
life. Here you can be yourselves, two people who love each
other. Here you can concentrate on one another's needs.

ANONYMOUS

It seems so very long ago, Lord,
when those wise words about a walled garden
were spoken to us
at our wedding.
At first it seemed to be the obvious thing to do.
Spending time with one another
away from the demands of others
was high on our agenda.
There was no doubt
that this was far more attractive
than working late,

calling friends,
or watching television.

We went into our "garden" often,
sharing secrets,
growing closer,
exploring life and love together.
Weekends back then
were full of fun and laughter
when we could wander hand in hand
beside the softly flowing river,
laughing at the raucous ducks
that squabbled, fought, and flapped
to get possession of our lunchtime scraps.

How things have changed.
For now our work-free days
are packed with plans and other people.
Conversation has become
a few lines
scribbled on a pad beside the phone,
or a terse message sent by text
while on the run.
The door into our garden is almost hidden
by rank weeds of busyness
and the demands of little children.

We claim we have no time, for we've forgotten.
Forgotten that love grows if it is tended,
and if neglected, dies.
So help us, Lord,
to once again make time for one another,

to listen and to talk about the things
that really matter
and are important to us both.
For I don't want to be
someone who's married to a stranger.
The other half of yet another silent couple
sitting in a restaurant,
with nothing new to say,
regarding time together as a duty,
or worst of all a painful waste of time.

I don't know if my husband
has thought about this garden much
in recent months.
So please help me to find the key
and, if need be, to oil the hinges.
Then perhaps we can both revel
in its beauty once again,
knowing the cultivation of our garden
is not a duty, but a critical investment.
An investment in our future
and the nurture of our love.

The Other Woman

~

You prepare a feast for me
in the presence of my enemies.
You honor me by anointing my head with oil.
My cup overflows with blessings.

PSALM 23:5 NLT

I said I'd never meet her, Lord.
Insisted that I utterly refused
to have a conversation with the woman
who had helped to wreck our marriage,
contributed to my lone parent status,
and caused our children
to live without the day-by-day relationship
that they should have, by right,
with both their parents.
The children were so loyal, Lord,
following my lead
and saying
that they had no desire to meet her either.

I thought I'd never have to face the meeting that I feared.
But when their father booked a holiday,
for two weeks in the sun,
which was a trip

that I could never give them,
I had a choice.
I could continue building
that wall around us
of hatred and despair,
or just accept our situation
and start to reconstruct
our lives,
embracing what I could not change
with all the grace that I could muster.

It wasn't easy, Lord.
You know how much I struggled
with my anger
and the longing
to turn back the clock
if only for our children's sake.
But when you whispered in my ear "forgive"
and "trust me, I will help you,"
you also gave me the strength to say,
"I will."

And, Lord it was OK!
When she arrived with my ex-husband
to pick up the children,
I had expected
to meet a glamorous and clever woman,
who'd make me seem so dull,
so plain and downright shabby
compared with her.
But Lord, it wasn't like that.
She seemed so ordinary and ill at ease

that I just couldn't hate her anymore.
All I could whisper
was "Father, forgive her"
and "help me to do the same."
And then you gave me peace.

It was the longest two weeks of my life, Lord.
And when the children bounded back to me,
suntanned and full of stories of all they'd done,
it wasn't easy to rejoice with them,
to keep my tongue in check
and to refuse to pry about the "other woman,"
asking them what she had said and done
with them and with their father.

They're happier now, dear Lord.
And we've established
a workable routine
of visits and of phone calls.
So maybe there is a crumbling of the walls,
and we can build a new and different family life.

It's not the one that I'd have chosen,
but at the very least please let it be
a life in which my children can grow up
as unharmed
as it is possible for them to be
by the mistakes and bad decisions
made by adults.
who now, whatever else they want in life,
still want the best for them.

I Thought He Was
THE ONE

It is not an enemy who taunts me—
I could bear that.
It is not my foes who so arrogantly insult me—
I could have hidden from them.
Instead, it is you—my equal,
my companion and close friend . . .
Morning, noon, and night
I cry out in my distress,
and the Lord hears my voice.

PSALM 55:12–17 NLT

~

You keep track of all my sorrows.
You have collected all my tears in your bottle.
You have recorded each one in your book.

PSALM 56:8 NLT

Dear Lord, I thought he was THE ONE.
I really did.
I felt that after all these years
of cautious steps toward a new relationship,
I'd met a man who loved me for myself.
I trusted him because he is your son,

and prayed that we'd enable one another
to heal past hurts,
put painful memories aside,
regain our confidence in other people,
and move with joy into the future you had planned.

But that, it seems, was not his vision.
So now I am alone again.
No, Lord, worse than alone,
because I miss the closeness that we shared,
and there's a raw and aching wound
in life and heart
and a void in my family.
For Lord, my children miss him too,
and wonder why he isn't here,
doesn't call,
and hasn't sent those funny little notes
for which they used to look
when he was out of town on business.

What makes it worse, dear Lord,
is that our town is small
and people notice.
They may not ask outright,
        "Have you split up?"
but I feel eyes upon me
when I walk into church,
and we're no longer there together.
I'm thankful that his job is taking him
a thousand miles away.
It's easier to say if asked,
"I couldn't take the kids away from school"

than to admit I got it wrong,
and that he never really loved me in the first place.

How will I face the future, Lord, without him?
They say that hearts don't really break,
but if that's so, then surely
my heart is the exception to that rule.
Oh help me, Lord.
Relieve this soul-destroying loneliness
and let me see a glimmer of your light
within the gloom of broken promises and loss of hope.
Give me a little confirmation
that promises you give within your Word
are true.
You really will not leave me or forsake me;
you do have good plans for my life.

One Day My Prince Will Come—Won't He?

Above all trust in the slow work of God.
We are, quite naturally, impatient in
everything to reach the end without delay.
We should like to skip the intermediate stages.
We are impatient of being on the way
to the unknown, something new . . .
Only God could say what this new spirit
gradually forming within you will be.
Give our Lord the benefit of believing
that his hand is leading you,
and accept the anxiety of feeling
yourself in suspense and incomplete.

PIERRE TEILHARD DE CHARDIN

~

Today I'll be at yet another wedding.
I think that is the third, dear Lord, this summer.
If things go on like this, I'm horribly afraid
that I will be the only one
without a husband,
or, as it is described
in this politically correct society of ours,
a partner or "significant other" in my life.

The element that's really different in today's event,
is that this marriage
has been arranged by the parents of the bride.
My friend was quite content
to let her family
introduce her to a man
they considered suitable,
and after quite a brief acquaintance,
she cheerfully agreed to marry him.

The custom seems unthinkable, dear Lord,
to Western minds.
Yet she insists that loving parents
are able to assess
what will be good for her,
and love can grow between a couple
as easily
after their marriage as before.

Can that be true, dear Lord?
You know that I have had
so many short-lived friendships,
and times when I was sure that I had met "my prince,"
only to have my heart
battered and broken once again,
so that these days I'm haunted by the fear
that my ideal does not exist
outside the pages of a sweet romance.

My friend says that she'd asked her parents
if they could find her
a husband who is handsome

and most important
a man of standing in their community.
And though, Lord, I am not so much concerned
with physical appearance,
I would like someone with a sense of humor,
for laughter oils so many squeaky wheels,
and a man who will connect with me
in mind and spirit.

Dear Lord, within the family of faith
there seems to be a shortage
of eligible men,
so maybe as I speak, he's not your child.
But you can draw him to yourself—
not merely for my sake, of course—
because marriages work best when both partners
have the same goals in life,
and if we're both your children,

God proves to be good to the man who passionately waits,
to the woman who diligently seeks.
It's a good thing to quietly hope,
quietly hope for help from God.
It's a good thing when you're young
to stick it out through the hard times.
When life is heavy and hard to take,
go off by yourself. Enter the silence.
Bow in prayer. Don't ask questions:
Wait for hope to appear.

LAMENTATIONS 3:25–29, *THE MESSAGE*

then we can serve your kingdom
and love you
with all our hearts.

As far as I'm aware, dear Lord,
there are no marriage brokers
within your church.
But if I trust you with my life,
then surely that includes the man I marry.
So from today I put the matter in your hands,
with just those few suggestions
about my ideal man,
and then I'll wait—I really will, dear Lord—
to see what you will do.

Loving through the Dark Days

"These two have come," he said, "to promise to face the future together, accepting what joy or sadness lies ahead . . . Nothing is easier than saying the words. Nothing is harder than living them out day after day . . . At the end of this ceremony, legally you will be man and wife, but still you must decide each day that you want to be married."

ARTHUR GORDON, "WEDDING BY THE SEA"

~

Love is not the feeling of a moment, but the conscious decision for a way of life.

ULRICH SCHAFFER

~

I take you . . . to have and to hold, for better, for worse, for richer, for poorer, in sickness and in health . . .

It seemed so easy then, dear Lord.
For we were young and very much in love.
To be together all our lives
was what we wanted above all things.
And we chose gladly
to make those vows
with due solemnity.

While those who loved us
looked on with joyful faces.

"I give you this ring," he said,
easing it across my knuckle
with care and tenderness.
"Wear it with love and joy.
I choose you to be my wife
this day and every day."
"I accept this ring," I said,
gazing into his eyes adoringly.
"I will wear it with love and joy.
I choose you to be my husband
this day and every day."

But now that day of love and laughter
is little more than distant memory.
For many years have passed
in which we've known
the usual pattern
of both joy and sorrow.
Days in which our wedding vows
have stood the test of time.

Of course we've had our ups and downs—
which of us has not—
but sitting in the doctor's office
I heard the words that from now on
will test our hearts' commitment to the limit.
For after many tests and long deliberation,
the doctor has come to share the news
that I have feared the most.

Dementia is the diagnosis for my husband, Lord.
A life sentence for both of us.

Oh help me, Lord!
You know that patience is a virtue
I often have in short supply.
How will I find my way
through all the rules and
    regulations
governing my access to the
    help
I'll surely need?
You know I'm not a nurse.
Will I be able
to understand the medication
and the treatment he'll
    require
for both his body and his mind?

How will I face the gradual loss of my beloved companion?
Not in one final parting
but day by day, week by week,
until he seems to be no longer
the man I love and married.

Please help him too.
For at the moment he is well aware
that memory plays cruel tricks,
and that he cannot always do the tasks
that once he found so easy.
Be with us as we grieve this loss together.
Help friends and family to understand

Our times are in His hand
who saith, "A whole I planned,
youth shows but half;
trust God: see all,
nor be afraid!"

ROBERT BROWNING

and to encourage us,
standing with us in the many ways
that we will need their help.

And most of all, dear Lord,
assure us both
that in this darkest of all valleys
we'll never be forsaken
but you will walk with us
right to the end.

A WOMAN AND HER CHILDREN

It is so hard to think that one small family
or even several generations
can really have an impact
on such a world as this,
where anger, pain, and downright wickedness
would seek to hold us prisoner.
We know that that we're not perfect.
Within our lives are so many places
that need God's healing touch.
And yet He has entrusted us with duties:
to love as He loves,
to serve, and to forgive,
so that we might be
a living demonstration of what a loving God can do
within and through the life of any family
that, trusting Him, is then prepared
for risky living.

 MARION STROUD

A Child's Eye View

~

"I sometimes wish," he sighed, as I whisked into the
bedroom to kiss him good night, "that you could be a
quiet country mother, and make cookies and knit!
But I suppose that would be against your nature."

"I want to be one like Mummy when
I grow up," she told them.
"What kind of a 'one' is that?" I asked, overhearing;
thinking of my profession, committees, hobbies, and interests.
"You know," she answered, "one that
cooks and cleans and kisses you better!"

"John's mother is a famous doctor now," he told me.
"Would you like it if I went back to work?" I asked him.
"I wouldn't mind," he said, considering
the matter, "if you were a secret agent!"

MARION STROUD

It's very hard to grasp, dear Lord,
how these three children seem to see
the ordinary mother that they share
as three entirely different women.
It shows how varied each of their needs are,

and as I tuck them into bed, I often ask myself
if I have skills enough to meet those needs
and whether I am in any way succeeding
at this important task that I've received from you.

Next week, next month, next year their needs may be
entirely different.
But will I recognize that fact?
And can I change and grow myself
in order to become the kind of mother
that they will need in days ahead?

When I lack wisdom, Lord, will you remind me
to ask of you?
Give me your listening ear
and most of all
your loving heart,
that sees the best in people—
    always.

Help me to hold my children
    in an open hand,
aware that they are
    individuals
created in your image,
cradled in my heart always
but not mine to possess.
And please help me, as their parent,
to teach and train consistently,
attending to their welfare
even though at times I feel
pressured by other demands.

> You will have more peace if you
> can grasp how . . . utterly safe
> it is to place your children in
> God's sure hands.
>
> JOHN WHITE

Help me raise them well
so that they grow, as Jesus did,
physically,
mentally,
socially, and spiritually,
and in favor
with God and man.

Night Watch

~

People who say they sleep like a baby
usually don't have one.

LEO J. BURKE

Dear Lord, you know I had a dream last night.
"Another baby on the way," they said.
And though
if I'm completely honest,
my spirit quietly shuddered
at the thought
of yet another little life for me to care for,
I was rejoicing too
because they said
that I must spend the next six months in bed.
Oh blissful thought!

I woke up almost disappointed.
I just don't want to leave my bed,
with grit-filled eyes and aching limbs,
to start this new and busy day
after another night of broken sleep.

You'd think that I'd be used to it by now
and able to survive
the waiting up for teenagers,

only to find when they get home,
our toddler son is ready for the day.

You know, dear Lord, I often long
for half his energy.
For he is like a human whirlwind,
racing through the day,
and still wakes in the early hours
to play.
If he were ill or cold or hungry
we could soothe him,
but he's just bored,
a little lonely,
and wide awake.

We've tried the remedies that they've suggested.
Bedtime routines,
toys in his bed,
a night-light in his room.
We've fed him, watered him, changed him,
picked him up, left him to cry,
and even, dare I say, in desperation,
brought him into our bed with us.
But still we keep night watch,
while all around
is wrapped in blissful, peaceful sleep.

Oh help us, Lord.
Help us to treasure
his glowing health,
boundless energy,
and endless curiosity.

And, Lord, be near to all those mothers
whose little ones
will never walk or talk like he does,
but still have to endure
the broken nights of sickness and distress.

Please give us stamina
and all the strength we'll need
for our day's work.
For we'll need focus and clear heads
as we face rush hour traffic
or operate machinery.

And Lord, we will need patience
for all the little problems
that loom so large when we are tired.
Hedge us round with wisdom,
so that we know
just how to meet
the challenge of demanding jobs
and all of our children's needs.

And most of all, dear Lord,
help us to cling to the assurance
that as with all of childhood's phases,
this too will pass,
and one night soon we'll all enjoy
some quiet, unbroken sleep.

On the Outside

~

I cannot even imagine where I would be today were it not for
that handful of friends who have given me a heart full of joy.
Let's face it, friends make life a lot more fun.

CHARLES R. SWINDOLL

Why, oh why, dear Lord,
are little girls so cruel to one another?
One day they're sharing secrets,
keeping seats for their "best friends,"
giving little gifts,
and ganging up against the world.
The next day they are
falling out,
closing ranks,
and excluding others.

Why is it that in any group there always seems to be
at least one who's left out?
This week it's my child on the outside.
She weeps
and I choke back tears on her behalf.
"Don't make me go to school tomorrow,"
she implores,
twisting tumbled curls through trembling fingers.
"I haven't got a partner for drama class.

Kate doesn't like me anymore;
I haven't any friends."

Why, Lord, must teachers let children
choose teams and partners?
Why don't they organize
the groupings for a change?
Surely they know how much negotiation
goes on behind the scenes.
And how the currency of fear manipulates:
friends trading favors,
begging for inclusion.
Have they forgotten
how much it hurts
to be the last one chosen?

Thank you, Lord, that for my child
this loneliness will be short-lived.
Usually she bounces off to school
anticipating the day that lies ahead
with joy.
While she is on the outside, Lord,
help her to learn from it.
To understand just how it feels
for those who're regularly
the odd ones out.
To discover that there is a need
to offer friendship
as well as to receive it.

She's sleeping now.
Please guard her dreams.
And as I send her off tomorrow,

help her to be assured
that she doesn't go alone
because she has your friendship.
Please be to her a warm and comforting reality,
offering friendship
that never wanes or wavers,
no matter what her day at school may bring.

Steps of Faith

Remember this! The Lord—and the Lord alone—is our God.
Love the Lord your God with all your heart, with all your soul,
and with all your strength. Never forget these commands that I
am giving you today. Teach them to your children . . . In times
to come your children will ask you, "Why did the Lord our God
command us to obey all these laws?" Then tell them . . .

DEUTERONOMY 6:4–7, 20–21, GOOD NEWS TRANSLATION

~

"You tell me all this about God," he said, five
years old and already a skeptic, "but how can I
know that you're right? What if there are other
gods . . . how will I know which one is true?"

MARION STROUD

Yes, Lord, there are so many other gods.
Gods that will invite my children's worship
silently, subtly, shaping desires
because their friends are bowing down
to money, popularity,
the latest toy or gadget,
the need to be
part of the "in-crowd."
Or, in these days of many faiths within our culture,
drawn to another god requiring

discipline and dedication,
a cause to live and die for,
which your church often falters to demand.

Lord, I can't with justice point the finger
when gods both seen and unseen
threaten
to steal my heart as well.
For I'm ashamed to say
I'm not immune
from loving what
    others have,
longing for power
    and influence,
and quietly pursuing
    my own agenda—
wrapped up in words
    like "service"
and "laying down
    my life."

Oh help me, Lord,
where I have moved
    away from solid rock
to shadowlands of compromise,
taking as my own
the standards of the world.
Return me to that sure foundation
on which I based my life at first.
Touch me afresh with hunger for
your Word,
fellowship with your people,

Many parents do nothing about their
children's religious education, telling them
that they can decide what they believe
when they're twenty-one. That's like telling
them that they can decide, when they're
twenty-one, whether or not they should
brush their teeth. By then, their teeth may
have fallen out. Likewise, their principles
and morality may also be non-existent.

PRINCESS GRACE OF MONACO

and messages from your Spirit.
And when I hear from you,
give me the courage to respond.

For then I can reach out
and teach my children with assurance
of an all-loving, all-knowing, and all-powerful God,
who perceives every concern within our hearts,
sees every step that we take,
and is ready to be found by everyone
who truly seeks Him.
I can teach them the facts,
model the love,
and seek to live out the implications,
but the final step of faith
is theirs to take, alone.

Don't forget what I teach you. Always remember
what I tell you to do . . . Trust in the Lord with all
your heart. Never rely on what you think you know.
Remember the Lord in everything you do, and he will
show you the right way. Never let yourself think that
you are wiser than you are; simply obey the Lord and
refuse to do wrong . . . When the Lord corrects you,
pay close attention and take it as a warning. The Lord
corrects those he loves, as parents correct a child of
whom they are proud.

PROVERBS 3:1–12,
GOOD NEWS TRANSLATION

Blended Families

*A father to the fatherless, a defender of
widows . . . God sets the lonely in families,
he leads forth the prisoners with singing.*

PSALM 68:5–6

~

"A town or family splintered by feuding will fall apart."

MATTHEW 12:25 NLT

~

*Be humble and gentle. Be patient with each other, making
allowance for each other's faults because of your love.*

EPHESIANS 4:2 NLT

~

*Children need quality time with their natural parent.
If Mom still goes to watch her son play football while
Dad takes his daughter to the movies, it gives the children
the sense that they are still important. But don't forget
to combine the group for a family outing. Also, parents
need some time together without the kids. Plan "date
night" for just the two of you once a week.*

Dear Lord, we were so glad when they got married,
blending two families
torn apart by death and infidelity

into one whole.
Foolishly perhaps,
we thought it would be easy
for them to become a family
especially when new babies came,
giving them children
that were no longer "yours" or "mine"
but "ours."

Sadly, Lord, that doesn't seem
    to be the case.
Our grandchildren still miss
    their father,
and "You can't tell me what to
    do,
you're not my mother"
falls easily from teenaged lips.

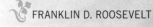

When you come to the end of
your rope, tie a knot and hang on.

FRANKLIN D. ROOSEVELT

Please help this family, Lord.
Give wisdom to both parents
and grace to understand
that styles of parenting can take a different path
through problems,
without the need to judge them
    right or wrong.

"As a mother comforts her
child, so will I comfort you."

ISAIAH 66:13

Please give them grace, Lord,
to keep their disagreements out
    of children's earshot
and to speak about the absent parent with respect.
Discussed, of course,
but privately
between themselves.

And when the loving feelings seem to founder,
help them to realize
that love is not so much a warm glow round the heart,
but a decision of the will
that must be made consciously
and lived out deliberately,
day after day after day after day.

Don't use foul or abusive language. Let everything you say be good and helpful, so that your words will be an encouragement to those who hear them . . . Get rid of all bitterness, rage, anger, harsh words, and slander, as well as all types of evil behavior. Instead, be kind to each other, tenderhearted, forgiving one another, just as God through Christ has forgiven you.

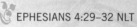 EPHESIANS 4:29–32 NLT

The Gift of Laughter

~

When the Lord brought back his exiles to Jerusalem,
it was like a dream!
We were filled with laughter,
and we sang for joy.
And the other nations said,
"What amazing things the Lord has done for them."
Yes, the Lord has done amazing things for us!
What joy!
Restore our fortunes, Lord,
as streams renew the desert.
Those who plant in tears
will harvest with shouts of joy.
They weep as they go to plant their seed,
but they sing as they return with the harvest.

PSALM 126 NLT

Dear Lord, today
the winner of the lottery
was interviewed on television.
And as the champagne corks flew high
and flashes from the cameras
lit up the scene,
they asked him what he'd buy
now that he'd never have to work again.

He spoke of gifts that he would give his children
of cars and houses
and exotic holidays,
and how I wish, dear Lord, that I could do the same.
If we have to be content
with fewer of life's material gifts,
living with furniture
that shows the wear and tear of family life
and spending our vacation here at home,
then, Lord, please, would you help us build a family
that's full of laughter?

You know that there are times
when I regard the glass you've handed me
as half empty rather than
half full.
But I don't want to be remembered as a mother
who snaps and snarls and grumbles
when things go wrong.
Help me to laugh, Lord,
when my mistakes—and
    those of others—
upset my plans.
Help me to see the funny
    side of life.

> A sense of humor can help you overlook the unattractive, tolerate the unpleasant, cope with the unexpected, and smile through the unbearable.
>
> BARBARA JOHNSON

And then, dear Lord,
help me to give my husband
    and my children
full attention
when they can't wait to share the latest joke,
or even take an age

to reach the punch line
of that old story that I've heard
a hundred times before.
Let me applaud them in my heart
as well as with my hands.
Help us to bless each other
with the sweet gift of laughter.

I know that we cannot expect
the sky
to be forever blue.
I recognize that there will be
dark storms of disappointment
and troubles
that will touch our lives
and are no laughing matter.
But with your help we won't be overcome
and we will say,
like Bible saints of old,
"The Lord has done amazing things for us.
What joy!"

Screens

*Fathers, do not aggravate your children,
or they will become discouraged.*
COLOSSIANS 3:21 NLT

~

*I think it is important to teach our children—
as the Bible says—line upon line, precept
upon precept, here a little, there a little. If
you try to teach a child too rapidly, much will be
lost. But the time for teaching and training is
preteen. When they reach their teenage
years, it's time to shut up and start listening.*
RUTH BELL GRAHAM

Dear Lord, there are some very difficult parental issues
that simply never feature
in biblical instructions
on how to raise our children.
Many of the problems that we grapple with today
are due to the technological advances
of the last ten years,
and now we have so little choice
but to embrace this new and different world
light-years away from all that we experienced
when we were young.

Right here and now,
the biggest subject of concern
and conversation
wherever parents gather
is technology,
that all-pervasive part of life
we sometimes simply refer to as "screens."
We worry, Lord, not just about the limits
that we should put on electronic games,
but how much time we should allow our children
in front of all the screens
that are as much a part of daily life for them
from infancy
as television was for us.

Of course it is quite true
that there is much of value to be found
from "Googling" the Internet
for information on school projects and the like.
But there are also terrifying traps
for the unwary.
Bullying on social media
can prompt electronic quarrels
that carry on quite viciously into the night,
and smartphones
that many children
seem to find necessary
to have close at all times
can be cause for mugging.

It doesn't end with phones
and access to the Internet, dear Lord.

Electronic games and TV shows
are available to children, it seems, from birth.
What kind of world are we creating?
Adults have to take their fair share
of the blame,
when we use television as a babysitter
so we can catch up on our chores,
or when we flop in front of any television program
because we are too tired to bother
finding better things to do.
And many of us spend our leisure hours
surfing the Net,
or let a ringtone from our phones
take precedence in any conversation.

Please help us, Lord.
Thank you for like-minded friends
with whom we can discuss
the issues that we face,
even if we find
we've different views on
    some things.
And when we've come to
    a conclusion
about what's right for us
and for our children,
give us the strength of
    character
to set a limit
on "screen time"
for everyone within the home.

Every word and deed of a parent is
a fiber woven into the character of
a child, which ultimately determines
how that child fits into the fabric of
society.

DAVID WILKERSON

Give us the discipline
to use the voice mail feature on our phones,
so that our meals can be a time
of uninterrupted conversation,
catching up on news
from school or work.
Help us to rediscover books and games
that we can sometimes share together
face-to-face,
while thanking you for all the many good things
that come into our lives—through screens!

The Trouble Tree

Ben was given a lift home by his employer after his van had broken down. The day had been full of petty annoyances on the job and Ben looked harassed and had little to say on the journey. But as he approached his front door, his boss noticed that the carpenter went up to a small tree . . . and held one of its lower branches briefly with both hands. Then he turned, gave a cheerful smile and opened the front door, scooping up two small children as he went in.

The next day the boss asked Ben what he'd been doing the night before. "I was hanging the troubles of my working day on my trouble tree," he replied with a grin. "They don't belong indoors. And when I collect them the next morning, it's amazing how many of them seem to have blown away."

FIONA CASTLE

~

Give all your worries and cares to
God, for he cares about you.

1 PETER 5:7 NLT

Dear Lord, I really think I need a "trouble tree."
For as you know I'm horribly prone
to bring the aggravations of my workday
back home with me.
I let them cluster on my horizon,

clouding my vision
so that I do not even notice
the burdens
that weigh my other family members down.

So just supposing
we all hung up our troubles at the door
and had a short time of transition,
changing our mind-set with our working clothes.
What a difference it would make
to dinnertime
if we could share the things
that pleased us from the day,
following the maxim
that food is best digested
when it's served seasoned
with peacefulness
and thanks.

And, Lord, I think we really need a trouble tree
close by the entrance to our church.

> Don't fret or worry. Instead of worrying,
> pray. Let petitions and praises shape your
> worries into prayers, letting God know your
> concerns. Before you know it, a sense of
> God's wholeness, everything coming together
> for good, will come and settle you down.
> It's wonderful what happens when Christ
> displaces worry at the center of your life.
>
> 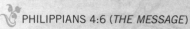 PHILIPPIANS 4:6 (*THE MESSAGE*)

For I—and many other mothers—
so often scramble in at the last minute,
ruffled by the stress
of getting children tubbed and scrubbed
and in their places,
feeling more like a single parent every week
because my husband often goes ahead
to give his time and energy in preparations
for the service.
Forgive me for my resentment, Lord,
but it is very hard to be serene and peaceful
when I am left to cope all on my own.

If I could leave my less-than-peaceful thoughts
hung up outside the church,
then maybe I would kneel to pray
and rise to worship
focused for once upon your glory and your grace,
rather than simply hurling
harassed petitions at your throne
and wondering
just what you have to say to me
to make things right this morning.

But Lord, you've just reminded me
that there's a trouble tree in place already.
Not outside the door but central to our vision
within the church.
Your cross,
where all our troubles
were laid upon your shoulders.
For it was there you carried

all our sins and sorrows
for time and for eternity,
and every day you have provided
the biggest trouble tree of all.

Lean on Me

Cast your cares on the Lord and he will sustain you.

Psalm 55:22

~

*Child of My love, lean hard, and let Me feel the pressure of
your care; I know your burden, child. I shaped it; balanced it
in Mine own hand; made no proportion in its weight to your
unaided strength, for even as I laid it on, I said, "I will be
near, and while she leans on Me, this burden will be Mine,
not hers; so will I keep My child within the circling arms of
My Own love." Here lay it down, nor fear to impose it on
a shoulder that upholds the government of worlds. Yet closer
come: You are not near enough. I would embrace your care; so
I might feel My child reclining on My breast. You love me, I
know. So then do not doubt; but loving Me, lean hard.*

Octavius Winslow

Today is such a hard day, Lord,
for in my heart of hearts,
I know that I have stumbled back
to where I started.
You know about this burden
that I have carried for so long.
This all-pervasive fearfulness
for one I love.

At times it seems I fear
more often and more strongly
than I love.

I thought that I had laid it down,
surrendered it to you,
tied it to your altar,
recognized that I can make an idol
out of love.
And for a while I felt released.

But now the same old problem
rears its ugly head again,
and my heart breaks afresh.
Dear Lord, I've talked to you
about this matter,
until I'm utterly devoid
of any other words to say.

My pain is great
because there is no way
that I can make it better for her.
And Lord, I'm shocked to say,
I even wish
that she could take the easy road
and have the thing she longs for,
although I know it wouldn't bring
the happiness for her
I long to see.

Some people say that prayer is never wasted.
That all of our requests
are tucked away

like ingots in the strongholds of Fort Knox.
In which case, Lord, my daughter must be
among the richest people in the world.

But actually I have to say
that for today
it's me, oh Lord,
standing in the need of prayer and comfort,
because I'm back to the temptation
to play God
in someone else's life.

And I'm so tired, Lord.
This burden is too hard for me to bear.
Please take it.
Help me to truly let it go,
to roll it on your shoulders once again.
And with my burden
please take me.

Please dry my tears.
Then hold me, Lord, against your heart
and let me hear your words again:
"Child of My love, lean hard."

Lost and Found

*Do not abandon yourself to despair. We are
the Easter people and hallelujah is our song.*

Pope John Paul II

~

*He is not here; he has risen, just as he said. Come and see the
place where he lay. Then go quickly and tell his disciples . . .*

Matthew 28:6–7

Dear Lord, they sent opinion pollsters
to ask why people thought
we celebrated Easter,
and I was horrified
to hear the vast majority had no idea
why we should have a holiday
at this particular time of year.

Admittedly some people mentioned lambs—
along with Easter bunnies—
but most assumed that Easter
is on the calendar
to celebrate that spring is on its way.
And they were glad
because they'd have some extra time
to get jobs done around the house
and garden.

And yet, Lord, I suppose
I shouldn't criticize them,
for though I knew what Easter was about,
it never touched my heart like Christmas
until that awful day when suddenly
my four-year-old was nowhere to be found,
lost among the throng of shoppers
in the department store.

It happened in an instant, Lord.
One moment I was chatting with a neighbor,
half-listening as our daughters
discussed the relative advantages
of chocolate eggs or bunnies
and tried to choose between them.
Then they crossed the aisle to look at dolls.
And when I turned to call them back,
she was gone.

I called her name,
trying to be calm
and telling myself
she couldn't have gone far.
My friend went one way, I another,
but it was as if the earth had opened up
and swallowed her.

With trembling legs and sweating palms
I pushed my way through crowds of shoppers,
screaming her name,
oblivious of curious looks
or of the fact

that I had sent a bright display
of Easter bunny Jell-O molds
rolling across the floor.
My frantic prayer was that you'd keep her safe
from kidnappers or worse,
when every other shopper now seemed to look like
an ax murderer!

I've never thought about
the pain and passion of the Easter story
in the same way
after that day, dear Lord.
For I had just an inkling
of what your heart must feel
as your beloved children wander
far away from you,
enticed by all the shiny things that this world offers.

You pursue us
with such relentless love
while we become distracted
by trifles, Lord.
And you don't merely call our names,
knock over merchandise,
or trample all else underfoot,
you sent your Son.

Did your heart break as He walked to Jerusalem
with flintlike face
to face the terror of the first Good Friday,
the silence of the intervening hours
before the glory of the Easter day,
and resurrection?

And does it break again
because in so-called Christian lands,
people don't know
that there's a way
for them to come back home to you?

Oh help us, Lord.
How dare we keep it to ourselves?
Help us to spread the joyful news
that death is truly vanquished,
sins can be forgiven,
and there's a road back home for everyone,
where from the greatest to the least
they'll all be welcomed in,
at Easter or at any other time.

A Different Kind of Prodigal

"I will not forget you! See, I have engraved you on the palms of my hands."

ISAIAH 49:15–16

~

Our children are loaned, not given to us, by God. We do our best to raise them to fear and love the Lord, but eventually we have to give them back to him. How they respond to God is not a total reflection on us. We do our best to be faithful, but we can't make their commitment to God for them.

MARSHALL SHELLEY

Dear Lord, he says that he has left the church,
abandoning the faith
that he professed from childhood.
He tells me that he cannot reconcile
a God of love
with all the suffering,
the wickedness and greed,
that stir his tender heart to anger
as he looks out upon the world
with adult eyes.

And yet it's hard to think that's he's a prodigal.
In many ways he is the son
of whom the most demanding parent would be proud.
He has done well at school,
his grades are all that we could hope for,
and now he's been sought out—
headhunted, as they say—
by a prestigious law firm,
where he will have bright prospects,
an income that will soon outstrip his father's,
and all that he could wish for
in the realm of life's material possessions.

I look at him today, dear Lord,
and tell myself
in many ways he hasn't changed.
He is still honest, keeps his promises,
is kind and caring
to animals, small children, and the elderly.
But life is centered now on different friends,
and other interests call for his allegiance.
Dear Lord, I am so sad when I observe
the absence of that spiritual dimension,
because he's turned his back
on his relationship with you.

I fear for him.
For now that he's no longer standing
on that firm rock of faith
and your forgiveness,
inevitably he's like a ship without an anchor,
so vulnerable
to all the pressures and temptations

that the fierce enemy of souls will hurl his way.
And my heart breaks.

I've wanted to confront him, Lord,
to argue in an effort to convince him
that he is wrong.
But I don't have the answers
    that he seeks
and as my husband says,
he must work through his
    doubts and questions
by himself.
For in the end,
it's only as your Spirit meets
    with his
that he'll be able to say once
    again
that he believes.

> "Restrain your voice from weeping
> and your eyes from tears,
> for your work will be rewarded,"
>   declares the Lord.
> "They will return from the land of the
>   enemy.
> So there is hope for your future . . .
> Your children will return to their own
>   land."
>
> JEREMIAH 31:16–17

One of his small rebellions
    as a teen, Lord,
was a tattoo.
A combination, so he said, of Chinese words
that speak of danger and of opportunity.
Today, Lord, you've reminded me
that you too have tattoos—
our names,
engraved upon your hands.
When you see them, you will remember
the least of these who wander, doubting.

Dear Lord, I can perceive this situation
as danger, fearing that it signifies

the end of his faith journey,
or as opportunity,
when he can seek out the truth for
    himself.
Then one day he can set his sights for
    home
and find his way back to you stronger
because of all he's learned and—yes—
    endured.
And in that way be much more able
to help your other children
who, like him, have blindly wandered
in that dark wilderness of doubt and disbelief.

A reminder to parents:
I didn't cause it.
I cannot control it.
Nor can I cure it.

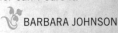 BARBARA JOHNSON

Someone Special

"Do not consider his appearance or his height . . . The Lord does not look at the things man looks at. Man looks at the outward appearance, but the Lord looks at the heart."

1 SAMUEL 16:7

~

I know that God will not give me anything I can't handle. I just wish he didn't trust me so much.

MOTHER TERESA

Today has been a special day, dear Lord.
Sunlit hours that we'll remember always.
For we've rejoiced together as a family
that we have reached the stage in life
when all our children
have finally completed their education.
Today we watched our youngest daughter
process in solemn convocation,
and then applauded
as she was given her degree.

Thank you, Lord,
for all the fun we've had along the way.
That we have learned so much
through teaching them.
And that we have been able

to celebrate with them
each little lesson learned
and hard-won honor,
knowing that one day
they'll stride into the future,
equipped and ready
to face the challenges of adult life.

But Lord, I think the moment I'll remember
with greatest clarity,
as I look back upon the high points of the day,
was when another mother
grasped my hand and said,
her face alight with pride,
"Please let me introduce you
to my son."

And as I looked for someone
wearing cap and gown,
or at the very least
a young man who could tease his sister
about the things she had achieved,
I realized she was leading me
toward a wheelchair,
and a young man,
whom superficially it seems
is most unlikely
to ever do the basic things
that independent living would demand.

I was so challenged, Lord,
because she had such joy in him.

There was no sense that this young man
was any less a person
than all the laughing throng
of able-bodied youngsters gathered around him,
or that he should be,
in any way,
considered second best.

As well as being challenged, Lord,
I was so humbled.
If it were me,
would I be able to take joy in such a child,
facing the future
with serenity and courage
as this brave woman does?
Or would I be full of fear,
wondering how we'd cope with growing older?

And in the secret places of my heart,
would I be harboring both anger and resentment
at what you had permitted, Lord,
or pitying myself
and mourning
the lack of future independence
for both of us?

Thank you that we can rejoice
about the things our children have achieved.
But please forgive us
if we have given them the false impression
that academic honors,
sporting prowess,

or even
a glittering career is all we care about.

For your Word tells us
that though it's good to use the gifts
with which you have entrusted us,
it's not the yardstick for success
in your economy,
for there is more to life than this.

Please help that mother, Lord.
Help all the parents of such challenged children,
whatever those challenges might be.
And help the children
to live their lives with pride and confidence
in who they are.

Then please enable all of us
to see them through your eyes,
for truly we're all equal in your sight,
and every one of us
is infinitely precious,
totally loved,
and absolutely valuable to you.

Not What I'd Have Chosen

~

Be glad, O people of Zion,
rejoice in the Lord your God . . .
"I will repay you for the years the locusts have eaten . . .
and you will praise the name of the Lord your God,
who has worked wonders for you."

JOEL 2:23–26

Dear Lord, you know that our beloved son has "married out."
I think that is the term that Jewish people use
when one of their religion
has found a partner
who is a Gentile.
And though our son is not a Jewish boy,
he's turned his face away
from Christianity,
the faith that he has known since childhood,
and found a wife
among those of another culture
whose wider family embraces a different faith.

You know our hearts are breaking
for so many reasons, Lord.
For there has been no wedding in our church
inviting you to bless this new relationship.

Instead their marriage was
conducted in a language
that we could not understand.
You know her parents were unhappy too, Lord,
and quite reluctant to allow the marriage,
which in their eyes
is just as undesirable
as the arrangement is to us.

But we have to accept
that what is done is done, Lord,
and thank you for the positives
within the situation.
Our son has now been given
a new experience of family life.
And though at first he found it
somewhat claustrophobic,
he now enjoys the closeness he's experienced
through his wife's family,
and believes it's something
to be desired and savored.
This is an interesting development considering
that for some while he has refused
to be a part of anything we do.

Thank you, Lord, that we have been accepted
within this group of people from another culture,
whose lives and worship would have been
a totally closed book
without this wedding.
Please help us to be equally
kind and accepting,
a witness of your love

to all of those
whose lives are now so closely linked to ours,
and who otherwise may not have met
real followers of yours.

You know, Lord, there are nights I really worry
about the influence that this religion
may have on any grandchildren
who will be born
to our son and his wife.
Thank you that her faith is nominal
and she has no desire to practice it.
And just as all our children
were dedicated
to you and to your service
when they were very young,
so we can pray for this new generation.
Help us to trust that you will give us opportunities
as they grow up
to tell them all about what we believe and why.

And then I must say thank you, Lord,
that though our son would try to shield his wife
from hearing
about our faith from us,
that she's intrigued and sometimes calls me,
using her cell phone to relieve the boredom
of business travel.
Sometime she asks what we believe,
quite open minded
about the differences that she observes
in our faith and her parents'.

Finally I want to thank you, Lord,
that you were present in that temple,
and when the bridegroom's party
was called upon to pray.
You spoke to me.
Thank you for showing me
the picture of a river,
initially flowing straight ahead
and then turning away,
meandering into a loop,
until it finally turned back
into the main flow once again.

As I wondered what this picture meant,
you whispered in my heart
that though my son appears to have abandoned
his childhood faith,
you have your hand on him.
And one day he'd be ready to return,
accept the truth of what he now denies,
and humbly bow before your throne again.

A Woman and Her Friends

I wish I had a magic formula for making friendship
*   happen. I don't . . .*
Friendship is not something about which we can learn
*   rules.*
Friendship and loving are arts,
* but not some kind of commercial art so that we can*
*   impress people.*
Friends are free individuals who risk being themselves
*   with one another—*
people who share their uniqueness and delight in seeing
*   each other*
and grow as a result of their shared relationship . . .
Without friends it is hard to be fully human.
We have to be, and to have, friends.

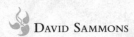 Ⅾᴀᴠɪᴅ Sᴀᴍᴍᴏɴs

Friends Near and Far

Friendship with oneself is all-important, because without it one cannot be friends with anyone else in the world.

ELEANOR ROOSEVELT

~

Friendship is not something about which we can learn rules . . . Friends are free individuals who risk being themselves with each other—people who share their uniqueness and delight in seeing one another grow as a result of their shared relationship.

DAVID SAMMONS

Dear Lord, it really is amazing
that I can have close friends
whom I have never met in person.
No loving hugs between us,
or cups of coffee
shared around the kitchen table,
while we off-load our worries
and talk about the issues
of daily life.

Using the wonders of the Internet,
my words can fly through cyberspace
and take me straight to countries

that I will never visit,
linking me with women
just like me at heart,
though outwardly
so very different.

We can share our lives,
"talking" with greater frankness
because misunderstanding
or falling out are far less likely
from a distance.
And after pouring out my heart,
I won't be faced with meeting
that person at the mall
and wishing that I'd been more reticent.

You know, dear Lord, that it is such a gift,
because you've made me one of those
who find it hard to feel at home
in crowds of people.
"Introvert," they label it,
meaning
I get my energy from times alone.
Yet I know
that as my online family develops,
it saves me from the struggle that I have
to make real friends
in daily life.

Dear Lord, I realize I still need other people.
For while I have this precious unseen family online,
unmet and yet such vital real–life friends,

they cannot know me warts and all.
So I still need to switch off my computer,
get out, and interact with other people
so that I'm part of flesh-and-blood community,
imperfect though it often is
and very hard to find.

So guide me, Lord.
Help me to take the first step,
reaching out my hand
without the anxious feeling
that I am being
assessed for what I have to offer,
measured for suitability,
weighed in the balances,
and perhaps found lacking.

Remind me that I need to give
as well as to receive
and be prepared
to be part of a team.
Help me to keep in mind
that you called twelve disciples,
not perfect people,
who were very different from one another.
Yet you entrusted them
with your life-giving message,
and as they worked together,
you changed the world.

You Never Bothered to Tell Me

~

Always be prepared to give an answer to everyone who asks you to give the reason for the hope that you have. But do this with gentleness and respect, keeping a clear conscience, so that those who speak maliciously against your good behavior in Christ may be ashamed of their slander.

1 PETER 3:15–16

I hadn't seen her for a long time, Lord,
that neighbor whom I noticed in the mall today
Pale, a little shaky on her feet,
and glad to stop and share a cup of coffee.
Three weeks in hospital, she said,
in pain and paralyzed with fear,
her days were just a blur of blood tests,
physical examinations,
and finally a major operation.

But Lord it wasn't this
that filled her conversation.
For someone in a nearby bed
had given her a booklet
that pointed her to you.

And she just bubbled over
with the joy of knowing
that she no longer has to face this trial alone.
"Do you know that Jesus loves you?
That you can be forgiven and that He wants to be your
    friend?"
she asked without a moment's hesitation,
her face alight with the sheer wonder of this fresh discovery.

When I said that I'd known it all since childhood,
she looked at me with wonder in her eyes.
"So are you saying," she asked, incredulous,
"that you have known this all along?
You've often knocked on my front door
to ask me to a bake sale,
or tell me of a special offer at the mall,
and yet you've never bothered
to share this most life-changing news of all?"

Dear Lord, you know that I am feeling
utterly ashamed.
But you know too, that sharing faith in you
is rarely done in our community,
where people all appear to have
such lovely homes, good jobs, and healthy children.
They seem to lack so little.
And even when they are in need,
the topics everyone avoids
are politics and faith.

On the odd occasions that I have tried to speak of you,
I just don't have the answers to their questions.

And so I pray
and hope that you will send somebody else.
Please help me, Lord.
Give me determination
to arm myself with knowledge and the willingness to share.

Please help me to remember
that all that you require of us
is that we're ready to explain
    when asked
the reason for the faith that
    we profess.
To say with confidence,
just as my neighbor did,
"This changed my life and I
    want you to know."
Not taking on responsibility for how my friends respond,
but knowing what it's like to be without you,
to be like one unworthy beggar enthusiastically
telling another who is starving
where he or she can find the bread of life.

How beautiful on the mountains
are the feet of the messenger who
bring good news, the good news
of peace and salvation.

ISAIAH 52:7 NLT

For Your Ears Only

*If anyone considers himself religious and yet does
not keep a tight rein on his tongue, he deceives
himself and his religion is worthless.*

JAMES 1:26

~

*Watch your tongue and keep your mouth
shut, and you will stay out of trouble.*

PROVERBS 21:23 NLT

Lord, I detest myself right now.
I passed along some information to a friend,
and though I told her she must keep it to herself,
that I was telling her in confidence
"So she could pray,"
she's told another member of our group.
Just like a forest fire,
the news has spread,
and now another friend has called to tell me
the selfsame thing "in confidence—
so I could pray."

Why did I do it, Lord?
I know that gossip isn't right.
But somehow it's so easy
to wrap it up in holy language

and use a prayer request as an excuse
to show that I am "in the know,"
"up with the information,"
"in touch with what's going on,"
"at the very heart of things"—
just like the friend with whom I shared it,
who loves to be the first one with
        the news.

What about the subject of our
        gossip, Lord?
How will she feel if she discovers
that she has been the topic of our
        conversation
and horrified concern—for weeks?
When she has taken all the care she can
to hide her heartbreak,
deep shame,
and what she sees
as her failure as a mother.

What can I do, Lord?
I long to call her up and ask for her
        forgiveness,
but that would be a terrible mistake.
She'd be so hurt, and feel betrayed—
she's such a private person.
And I am very much afraid that our relationship
would then be wrecked beyond repair.
No, all that I can do is ask for your forgiveness,
refuse to feed the gossipmongers
any additional ammunition,

> The one who is absent should
> be safe among those who are
> present.
>
> ANONYMOUS

> Nothing is opened in error
> more than the mouth.
>
> ANONYMOUS

and avoid speculation
or the criticism
that in some twisted way makes us feel better,
priding ourselves that in this circumstance at least,
somebody else is faring worse than we are.

And for my friend I pray, dear Lord.
Help her, bless her, strengthen her.
Don't let her know that we have talked
of her affairs.
Show me how to comfort her without intruding,
listen to her with full attention if she wants to talk,
and never again share news
that is not mine,
with anyone at all, "just for their prayers."

Fine Feathers

The finest clothing made is a person's own skin, but, of course, society demands something more than this.

MARK TWAIN

~

If most of us are ashamed of shabby clothes and shoddy furniture, let us be more ashamed of shabby ideas and shoddy philosophies . . . It would be a sad situation if the wrapper were better than the meat wrapped inside it.

ALBERT EINSTEIN

~

People seldom notice old clothes if you wear a big smile.

LEE MILDON

"I've just been shopping for my Christmas cruise,"
   she told me,
tossing carrier bags and tissue paper
onto the bed
with casual carelessness.
"But what about the clothes you bought last year?" I asked,
glancing at her closet,
which was already bulging
with brightly colored leisure wear.
"I couldn't wear those things again," she said.

"I'm travelling with lots of people
who were on board last time.
You simply can't be seen in the same outfit twice."

Dear Lord, why is it
that we become so very anxious
about the clothes we wear
and how we look?
I really cannot criticize my friend,
for I've just left the hairdresser,
where my unruly locks were
colored, curled, and blow-dried into shape.
I was seeking confidence in someone else's touch
because I have important meetings to attend
tomorrow.

And as the school year starts again,
statistics say that the majority of mothers
are busy shopping for a trendy outfit,
in which they will accompany
their child to school.
They're spending freely
because they are so scared of being less
up-to-the-moment, confident, and smart
than other "yummy mummies."

Oh help us, Lord,
When all creation
speaks of beauty and design,
I'm sure you're glad to see your people
enjoy those special skills that stylists have
in making lovely things.

And you must be pleased
when your people take time
to care for their own bodies,
recognizing
that they are your temple.

But that is such a small part of the whole
that makes us lovely in your sight.
And if we make appearance more important
than being loving, joyful, peaceful,
patient, kind, and good,
we miss the point
of what you value.

One day, the Bible tells us,
we'll all have special robes to wear.
And in the meantime, Lord,
help us to guard our thoughts and motivation.
Please keep us free from worry
about the way we look
or what we have to
    wear,
and turn much more
    of our attention
to what you see
when your gaze falls
upon our hearts.

"That is why I tell you not to worry about
everyday life—whether you have enough
food and drink, or enough clothes to wear
. . . Why worry about your clothing? Look
at the lilies of the field and how they grow.
They don't work or make their clothing, yet
Solomon in all his glory was not dressed
as beautifully as they are. And if God
cares so wonderfully for the wildflowers
. . . he will certainly care for you."

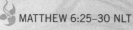 MATTHEW 6:25–30 NLT

139

Gray Days

~

No fears I need deliverance from today,
but nothingness.
No rain, no sun,
no energy,
and yet no weariness from work well done;
no joy and yet no sadness deep
as I look out upon the world.
It all seems fast asleep.
No laughter, yet no tears,
no wind to stir the leaves,
no reason why my heart should grieve,
November.

MARION STROUD

Dear Lord, you know I struggle
with November,
and all the other winter days
when in the house and office,
it's hard to see without electric light,
even by morning coffee break or in the afternoon.
And if I do work up the energy to venture out,
the skies are gray,
the leaves no longer rustle underfoot
but lie in soggy heaps,

and the bright lights of Christmas
remind me that longer days
are still far away.

It's on these days, dear Lord,
that I feel of such little use to anyone,
and I really wonder
if the small things that I do,
which on the gray days seem so meaningless
and unimportant,
can possibly have value
in the eternal scheme of things.
And with those thoughts flood in the doubts
about the reason that I'm here,
and what this life is all about.
And worse,
you seem a million miles away.

Thank you, Lord, for friends
who do not suffer from gray moods.
They cheerfully point out
the beauty of the winter days,
where nature is still full of
    interest
though found
in shades of black and white
    and gray.
Friends who celebrate the
    chance
to curl up cozily
with book or knitting pins
beside a dancing fire,

My heart is steadfast, O God . . .
I will sing and make music.
Awake, my soul!
Awake, harp and lyre!
I will awaken the dawn.

PSALM 57:7–8

relishing the opportunity
of a few fallow weeks
before the busyness begins again.

And thank you even more, dear Lord,
for those who share this seasonal depression,
but who have learned
a better way to cope with it.
Thank you for a listening ear.
A friend who doesn't try to "fix" me
but listens quietly
while I pour out my heart,
and then lights candles,
puts on upbeat music,
and celebrates that we are friends
with dainty china and delicious cake.

Thank you, Lord, for her reminder,
that whether those around me see
what I'm contributing
to your economy
as valuable or not,
and even if I think I
    should do something
bigger, better,
what some might
    think of as "more
    spiritual,"
the best gift I can give
    the world
is me.

If I say, "Surely the darkness will hide me
and the light become night around me,"
even the darkness will not be dark to you;
the night will shine like the day,
for darkness is as light to you.

PSALM 139:11–12

I may be messy,
forgetful, impulsive, and imperfect,
but I am "made new by your grace."
When you made me,
you threw away the mold,
and there is absolutely no one who
can take my place.

How long, O Lord? Will you forget me forever?
How long will you hide your face from me?
How long must I wrestle with my thoughts
and every day have sorrow in my heart?
How long will my enemy triumph over me? . . .
My foes will rejoice when I fall.
But I trust in your unfailing love;
my heart rejoices in your salvation.
I will sing to the Lord,
for he has been good to me.

PSALM 13:1–6

Speaking of the Unspeakable

Happy families are all alike; every unhappy family is unhappy in its own way.

LEO TOLSTOY

~

The Lord is close to the brokenhearted;
he rescues those whose spirits are crushed.

PSALM 34:18 NLT

Dear Lord, I really don't know what to do,
for I'd believed
that things like this don't happen
within the neat and tidy houses
of our quiet suburban street.
When my friend rang the doorbell
as I was serving lunch,
I thought she'd come to leave a key
for the delivery man.
I certainly did not expect she'd fall into my arms,
face blotched with tears,
saying her husband had hit her yet again.

Outwardly they're just like many other families
of my acquaintance.

A lovely home and two cars in the garage,
two healthy little boys,
income from a good professional job.
Dear Lord, what possible excuse is there
for him to batter her like that?

On this occasion
the trigger was her toddler,
who'd found some scissors
and had snipped the fringe along the bottom of the sofa
while she was busy in the kitchen.
But my friend says that it can be the smallest thing
that sends him into a rage.
And after he has beaten her,
he wrecks the house as he had done today,
pouring cooking oil onto her clothes,
and then making sure she cannot wash them
by leaving
the washing machine in pieces on the floor.

As far as I can see, dear Lord,
domestic violence is a secret shame.
It's not an issue that is talked about
where women gather.
And I don't think I've ever heard a sermon
that addresses
men who act like this,
although your Word has much to say
about the way that husbands should treat their wives.

The trouble is that neither my friend nor her husband
believe in you
except in a vague, general way

of "somebody up there,"
a kindly Father Christmas figure.
So she wouldn't think
of asking you for help.

But help she surely needs.
For neither parents nor her in-laws
are prepared to get involved.
Indeed, her husband's mother has accused her
of trying to cause trouble for her son,
when she found out my friend had finally confided
in someone from outside the family.

Dear Lord, my instinct was to urge her
to leave this man,
who has ill treated her for years.
But she says she has nowhere else to go,
no way she can support her sons,
who even now are liable to hit her
when she brings discipline into their lives.

At the moment all that I can do, it seems,
is pray for her
and tell her that she's infinitely precious
and beloved by you.
I can also be a listening ear
and encourage her to seek some help
from people who can show her
she has options and ways out
of this abusive situation.

And though I'll do it through my gritted teeth, dear Lord,
I'll pray
that you'll confront her husband,
because weird though it seems to me,
you love him too.

If You Want to Walk on Water . . .

*During the fourth watch of the night Jesus went out
to them, walking on the lake. When the disciples saw
him . . . they were terrified . . . Jesus immediately
said to them: "Take courage! It is I. Don't be afraid."
"Lord, if it's you," Peter replied, "tell
me to come to you on the water."
"Come," he said.*

MATTHEW 14:25–29

~

They all alike began to make excuses.

LUKE 14:18

~

*If you really want to do something, you'll find
a way. If you don't, you'll find an excuse.*

ANONYMOUS

Dear Lord, I'm full of admiration for my friend.
For at the age when many women
assume that they'll be occupying
an "empty nest"
and living at a slower pace,

even if
they haven't actually retired,
my friend is giving up a year
to short-term mission,
where she will be the oldest volunteer by far.

She'd always dreamed of serving you full-time, Lord.
But growing up
her parents made it very clear
that ordinary folk
could not expect "dreams to come true."
They believed
that few of us will get to live
beyond the boundaries of nine to five.
So she assumed
that following her dream was not for her.

She says that she was very much aware
of the big gaps in her education
and felt she didn't have the brains
to learn about theology,
write essays,
or do all the things
that she assumed she'd have
    to do
before she could be
used by you in your church.

> It's never too late to be what
> you might have been.
>
> GEORGE ELIOT

Even when these fears were calmed,
she thought that she was far too old
to take the risk of being asked
to do things outside her comfort zone.

Her year was still
too full of obligations
for her to listen when you called her
to what, for her, would be
that extraordinary feat
of water walking.

But then her husband pointed out
that in twelve months,
she'd have lived another year,
and so she might as well
say with Peter,
"Lord if it is you . . ."
Then having heard His "come,"
get on with it,
leaving her fears behind her in the boat.

Dear Lord, please help me learn from her example.
For I so often hesitate
until the opportunity has passed me by.
Like her,
I think if I can't guarantee the
    outcome
it's probably advisable
to stay there in the boat.
Or if the timing isn't right in my
    opinion,
the task too insignificant,
or barriers stand in my way,
I shrug my shoulders
and tell myself I must have been mistaken
in thinking that I heard your voice.

In this life we cannot do great
things. We can only do small
things with great love.

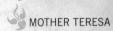 MOTHER TERESA

Remind me, Lord,
that willingness is all you ask for,
and that I really have a choice.
Peter was the only one
who left the safety of the fishing boat,
but others could have made the
    same request.
And if you call,
then I can join the company of
    water walkers,
because when you give the
    command,
you'll also undertake
for all the challenges
that follow.

Everything is risky . . . [A] half-
million Americans . . . require
emergency room treatment
each year for injuries sustained
while falling out of bed.

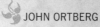 JOHN ORTBERG

Will Someone
Please Carry Me?

*A friend is someone who knows all
about you and loves you just the same.*

ELBERT HUBBARD

~

*Friendship is a living thing that lasts only as long as it is
nourished with kindness, sympathy, and understanding.*

MARY LOU RETTON

~

Cast all your anxiety on him because he cares for you.

1 PETER 5:7

When we were children, Lord,
we'd ask our friends,
"Are you a PLP?"
And if they answered yes,
we'd lay our full weight on them
with screams of laughter,
claiming that they were
a Public Leaning Post.
Little did I think, dear Lord,
that I would still be acting out that game in adulthood.

Habit makes it hard, dear Lord,
to shed the image
of being someone
whom everyone expects
to deal with all life brings her way,
as well as being constantly available
to lift the load
from other people's shoulders.

Perhaps it is my own fault, Lord,
for putting on the mask of competence
and coping,
so that when people ask me how I am,
I automatically say "fine" because
that's what they all seem to expect,
when underneath,
I am longing
to share my burden
with someone else.

Please help me, Lord,
to trust
that when my friends ask how I am,
they really want to know.
Give me the courage to be vulnerable
and shed for once
the Mrs. Fix-it mantle
that I am prone to wear,
because it is expected of me.

Perhaps, Lord, I am suffering
from a distorted form of pride.
And so by carefully keeping

my cloak of competence in place,
I'm robbing others of the opportunity
to offer what they'd really love to give,
if I would share
how I was feeling.

And help me, Lord,
to let what I have learned
make me more sensitive
to the unspoken messages
our body language gives.
For there are times
when I am guilty
of going through the motions of concern,
while car keys in my hand
and eyes that wander
suggest that I just want the easy answer of
"I'm fine."

This is a tricky area
of human interaction,
and I'm so very thankful, Lord,
that other people's well-being
does not depend on me
to get it right.

Thank you that you're there for all your children,
and you invite us
to cast all our concerns, our joys, and sorrows
on your broad shoulders,
for you're the tireless burden bearer
for us all.

Love in Action

*Friends always show their love. What are
relatives for if not to share trouble?*
PROVERBS 17:17, GOOD NEWS TRANSLATION

~

*The friend who can be silent with us in a moment of
despair or confusion, who can stay with us in an hour of
grief and bereavement, who can tolerate not knowing, not
curing, not healing . . . that is a friend who cares.*

HENRI NOUWEN

So many people wrote or telephoned, dear Lord,
when news of my bereavement was announced
at church and in the local papers,
and I am grateful for them all.
It cheered my heart to learn
of incidents that took place in my mother's early life
and all the little things she'd done
for other people
of which I'd never heard.

I thank you for them, Lord,
even those well-meaning folks
who tried to find a reason in your economy
for my mother's early death,
exhorting me to praise you

in the face of all the heartbreak,
and filling the silences between us
with pious platitudes.
Because in their own desperate need
to "fix me,"
they could not bear to simply sit
and hold me while I wept.

"If there is anything that we can help you with," they said,
"anything at all . . .
don't hesitate to ask."
So kindly meant,
these offers,
but since I really didn't know
just what they had in mind,
and it was too hard to think
of what jobs to offer,
I just smiled and thanked them,
struggling numbly on.

> Lots of people want to ride with you in the limo, but what you want is someone who will take the bus with you when the limo breaks down.
>
> OPRAH WINFREY

Dear Lord, I want to praise you
 for the precious few
who turned up on the doorstep unannounced,
bringing little but themselves—
no answers,
no need to know the details of my mother's tragic accident,
ready to sit with me in silence,
care for my children,
or take me to the supermarket.
Just showing love,
that could be touched or felt,
with a toolbox or a tin of cakes.

And so through these last long weeks,
my ancient car has been kept on the road
and my home has gleamed with polish
under the tender care of those
who love to make a house a home,
while I've embarked on all the extra duties
that sudden death brings in its wake,
comforted
not so much by hearing words but by seeing love,
for love in action is surely
love made visible.

Don't walk in front of me, I may not
  follow.
Don't walk behind me, I may not lead.
Just walk beside me and be my friend.

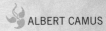 ALBERT CAMUS

A Woman at Work

Everyone can do something beautiful for God.

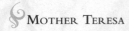MOTHER TERESA

*Work can bring so much pleasure and purpose to
life—it gives us the sacred opportunity and privilege
to change the world around us a little bit for the better.
Abraham Lincoln said, "Most people are about as happy
as they make up their minds to be." I believe we can
figure out a way to enjoy whatever job we are working at.*

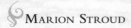MARION STROUD

*Never tire of doing even the smallest things for Him,
because He isn't impressed so much with the dimensions
of our work as with the love in which it is done.*

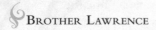BROTHER LAWRENCE

Monday Morning Musings

The faithful love of the Lord never ends!
His mercies never cease.
Great is his faithfulness; his mercies
begin afresh each morning.

LAMENTATIONS 3:22–23 NLT

~

My heart is confident in you, O God;
my heart is confident.
No wonder I can sing your praises!
Wake up, my heart! . . .
I will wake the dawn with my song.

PSALM 57:7–8 NLT

Dear Lord, today is Monday,
and when I stop to think about the week ahead,
it's easy to feel overwhelmed:
heart sinking,
stomach churning,
doubt rising
as to how I will begin to cope with all I have to do.
I feel as if I have a swarm of worries
swirling through my mind like angry bees.

But Lord, I really do not want to be
a Monday morning moaner.
So help me, please,
to have a different attitude.
For while, perhaps, I cannot choose
the routine tasks
that fill my hours,
it's possible to change the time I spend on each
and to decide how I will tackle them.
I am a sculptor, with the power to shape my day.

So help me, Lord, this working week
to step into today
and every day with you,
remembering that I can grumble
because I have to go to work
or I can praise you because I
     have a job.
And if the rain streams down my
     window,
I can complain about wet
     Monday mornings
or note with thankfulness that my plants are being watered,
and pray for those who haven't seen a drop of rain
for years.

As well as work that pays the bills, Lord,
there's care of home and family
that keeps me on my feet till late at night.
You know that sometimes I'm so weary
I cut the corners,
impatiently,

> Two men looked out through
>   prison bars.
> One saw mud, the other stars.
>
> ANONYMOUS

longing with every fiber of my being
to reach that glorious moment
when I have finished
and can sit down and have some peace.

But this week, Lord enable me
to cherish
my children's bath time,
the bubbles and the splashing,
patting their bodies dry with fluffy towels.
And then the moment after prayers and bedtime stories
when they might whisper little secrets
made safe to share by darkness.
Remind me, Lord,
that these children are your special gifts,
lent to me for a few short years.
Help me to care for each of them
according to their needs,
not my ideas of how a child should be.
And grant me special patience
with individuals who demonstrate my faults
because they share my genes,
and in their attitude toward life are just like me!

Any fact facing us is not as important as our
attitude toward it, for that determines our
success or failure. The way you think about
a fact may defeat you before you ever do
anything about it. You are overcome by the
fact because you think you are.

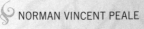 NORMAN VINCENT PEALE

Whatever gifts or graces I may lack, Lord,
there are those precious things called options,
which neither friends nor enemies can take away.
For I can choose my attitude
today and every day,
knowing that with that choice comes freedom
and the ability to soar on wings as eagles,
to run and not be weary,
to walk and not faint.

It Wasn't on the List

The key to being organized is making lists—
or that is what they tell me, Lord.
And so I've tried to keep a handle on my life
with pocket calendars, work organizers,
electronic gizmos, and the plain old knot
tied in a hanky if I have one.
All this just for the sake of bringing order to my days
and generating
that glow of satisfaction
when item after item is deleted
or crossed off the page.

But Lord, these lists can have a darker side.
For on the days when people take the time
that's neatly scheduled
for something else,

I feel as if I have a tyrant whispering in my ear,
accusing me of slackness,
wrong priorities,
and failing to complete essential tasks.
When actually, dear Lord,
all that has happened
is that I have allowed your needy people
to take the place of my agenda.

The Gospels tell me, Jesus,
that it was your custom
to plan your days before first light
in prayer.
But even though you had a sense of purpose,
it never stopped you
from pausing on the road,
healing blind beggars,
responding to a frantic father's cry for help,
or sharing food
with that despised and hated tax man.

So as I start another day, dear Lord,
please help me.
Enable me to use the gadgets and the systems well
to keep on top of texts and everlasting e-mails,
and help me not to dismiss
the calls that will demand my time.
Yet keep me ever open
to the nudges of your Spirit
to notice someone who requires
your loving touch.

For Lord, I know that while it's nice to be important,
it's so much more important to be nice.
So may I never be like priest or Levite,
passing swiftly by upon the other side,
focused—or blind,
afraid of being open to attack themselves
or simply short of pity.[2]

For I remember
that though your Word may never mention "lists,"
you notice when a tiny sparrow falls.
And inasmuch
as I might offer help to anyone,
significant or stranger, rich or poor,
you see it as an offering to you.

Reaching My Limit

There is a time for everything,
and a season for every activity under heaven.

ECCLESIASTES 3:1

~

When it's time for me to walk away from something
I walk away from it. My mind, my body, my
conscience tell me that enough is enough.

JERRY WEST

~

I have had enough.

GOLDA MEIR

Dear Lord, I really should be going home.
The day has hurtled by
and though I reached my desk
before my team
and worked through lunch,
I still am nowhere near the end
of all the things
I set myself to do today.

The trouble is
that in the working culture of this firm,
you're judged

not by the quality of work that you produce,
but by time spent in the office,
or your availability on cell or smartphone
seven days a week.
And if you hint you're limited
by needs of home or family,
you're seen as weak, inadequate, and liable
to lose your job.

Well, much as I may hate to say it, Lord,
I've had enough.
There'll always be more
e-mails needing answers,
people to call,
colleagues to interact with.
My husband and my children
    need me
and I need
to put a limit on my working day.

> Do what you can, with what
> you have, where you are.
>
> TEDDY ROOSEVELT

Help me, dear Lord,
to recognize that if I died tonight,
the world of work would carry on
without me.
Give me the courage
to list the jobs that I must do tomorrow,
close my computer,
clear my desk,
and then go home,
confident that I have done the best I can today
and now it's time to stop.

Teachers

If a doctor, lawyer, or dentist had 40 people in his [or her] office at one time, all of whom had different needs, and some of whom didn't want to be there and were causing trouble, and the doctor, lawyer, or dentist, without assistance, had to treat them all with professional excellence for nine months, then he [or she] might have some conception of the classroom teacher's job.

DONALD D. QUINN

~

Not many of you should presume to be teachers, my brothers, because you know that we who teach will be judged more strictly.

JAMES 3:1

Dear Lord, it's Parent-Teacher Consultation Day,
and as I go to school and hear
how my child's getting on,
I want to talk to you
about her teachers.
They have such influence
upon their students' lives,
and at a certain stage
when children switch allegiance
from "what my mommy says"
to "well, my teacher tells us"

it really seems their power
is absolute.

It's not an easy job, Lord,
and pay is modest
for all the time they spend
both in the classroom and at
    home
in preparation.
And these days there must be considerable pressure
to "teach to tests"
rather than to focus on
the individuality of every child
and concentrate
on opening hearts and minds
to the exciting possibilities of learning.

Promote the kind of living that
reflects wholesome teaching.

TITUS 2:1 NLT

Of course I hope I'll get a good report,
be told she's doing well,
cooperates with others,
and is a joy to teach.
But if there are some teachers
with whom she doesn't work so happily,
help me to differentiate
between a clash of personalities—
for there are one or two she tells me that she hates—
and my child's lack of understanding or ability.
Help us to approach the situation calmly
and work together to remedy it.

Thank you, Lord, that my child
is able to attend a well-run school
full of children whose parents

share my aspirations,
wanting children to grow into well-adjusted people
who'll make a contribution
to our society.
In general we're all supportive
of the school community,
wanting to help in every way we can.

But Lord, what a huge challenge it must be
to teach in schools where pupils must be searched
for deadly weapons
before the school day can commence.
Where there is almost no respect
for people in authority,
and expectations are so low
that just to teach a child to read and write
is now considered
a great achievement.
Please be with these brave people
who wage war on ignorance and shape young lives
that have already seen too much of poverty
in every aspect
of their growing up.

And Lord, while I am on the
    subject
of teachers,
I don't want to forget that band
    of faithful people
who teach my child
in Sunday school.
No pay for them
and yet there is considerable commitment

> If you have knowledge, let
> others light their candles at it.
>
> THOMAS FULLER

week after week.
These great people,
who may not even have kids of their own,
can shape our children's view of you
to such a large extent.
Please bless them, Lord.
And help me to encourage them,
recognize their special qualities,
and thank them
for all the precious time and energy they give my child.

Of course not every child is educated
within the public system,
so please, Lord, bless and help those parents
who have decided
to teach their children
within the homeschooling community.
It can't be easy
to be both mother and a teacher
who's with her pupils
every hour of every day.

So help them, Lord.
Help them to live out their faith honestly
within a situation where patience
can be stretched to the breaking point.
And please give all our teachers
the skills and insight that they need
as they equip our children
for life in such a complex world,
enabling them to be the people
that you've created them to be
in such a time as this.

Housework

To give our Lord a perfect hospitality,
Mary and Martha must combine.

TERESA OF AVILA

~

It is most laudable in a . . . woman to be devout, but she
must never forget that she is a housewife; and sometimes she
must leave God at the altar to find him in her housekeeping.

BERNADINE OF SIENA

~

Whatever your hand finds to do, do it with all your might.

ECCLESIASTES 9:10

It simply isn't possible to put it off again, Lord.
I can't see through the windows
and the dust
is gradually collecting on the carpet,
making that shade of harebell blue
chosen with such care
start to resemble
a gray November day.
We're entertaining visitors tomorrow, Lord,
and though I've got a lot of other things to do,
today I simply have to clean the house.

Thank you, Lord,
that I am blessed enough to own a home.
You have provided work
from which we earn enough to pay the mortgage.
And though we don't possess the most
    updated version
of every gadget known to man
and our furniture
shows the wear and tear of lively children,
pets, and visitors,
when strangers ask us where we live,
we can reply like you did, Lord:
"Come and see."[3]

Thank you for this kitchen, Lord.
The hub of every home, they say,
and certainly a place where I have spent
a large proportion of my month.
Thank you that we have food enough.
Although I sometimes grumble inwardly
that I'm the one
who makes the meals,
at least my family goes to bed well fed,
and dirty plates proclaim their healthy appetites.

Now, Lord, I have to bravely take a step
into quite alien territory.
For though in theory the children are responsible
to tidy up their rooms
and put their dirty clothes into the hamper,
unless I venture in there occasionally,
I fear we'd be liable to get a visit

from the department
of health and safety!

As I draw back the curtains
and open tight-shut windows
to summer's freshening breeze,
I'd ask that you would make your
   sunshine
stream brightly
into my son's heart.
Help him to bring into the light
any areas
that need your cleansing touch,
just as I whisk away these smelly football socks
and move a dirty cereal bowl
from underneath the heap of blankets
on the floor.

My daughters' rooms are sweeter smelling, Lord.
And as I dust those little gifts
bestowed by friends
and marvel
at the many aids to beauty
they think they need at such a tender age,
I pray that you will bless
all their relationships
and give them helpful friends
who will encourage them to walk with you.

And finally, dear Lord, there is our bedroom.
Thank you for peaceful sleep.
We're grateful that we have this quiet place

This house is protected by
killer dust bunnies.

ANONYMOUS

where we can share our minds, our hearts,
our bodies, and our prayers.
Help us to keep all anger,
cares, and disappointment
shut firmly
outside the door.
Fill the room with your love,
    your peace, your joy,
so that within its walls
we'll be reenergized and
    reequipped
to face the world.

Housework is what a woman does
that nobody notices unless she
hasn't done it.

 EVAN ESAR

Butterflies

The father of chaos theory, meteorologist Edward Lorenz, described how tiny changes in initial atmospheric conditions, such as the flap of a butterfly's wings, can alter weather patterns several weeks later on another continent. This is known as the butterfly effect.[4]

~

Who despises the day of small things?
ZECHARIAH 4:10

Dear Lord, so many things
that I am asked to do at work
seem to have so little likelihood
of being used by you
that is it hard to look upon the job I do
as being part of your eternal plan.

And yet we're told that butterflies can make a difference
on weather patterns miles away,
hard though that may be to believe,
and that we should never
discount the small things that we do,
if we take care to do them for your sake.

So, Lord, as I set off to work today,
please help me to go expectantly,
recognizing,

that for this time at least,
my routine job is
that small corner of your kingdom
that you've reserved for me.
For it is true that no one else
has precisely my contacts,
opportunities, or gifts
to labor for you there.

Help me to do all that I do,
however seemingly mundane,
with care and thoroughness,
keeping alert
for opportunities to speak of you,
and being ready at all times
to explain clearly—if they should ask—
the reason for believing as I do,
explaining both gently
and with respect.

You know it isn't always easy, Lord,
to be part of the social scene at work.
What do I do about the jokes,
the gossip, and the casual attitude
to the firm's property,
in which I really cannot be involved?
And yet it's harder still
to separate myself
without appearing to be prim or disapproving.

You know there is a culture in the office
that it is only necessary to bother about
timekeeping or productivity

if you want to be noticed.
So when I'm working hard
they say that I'm intending
to catch the boss's eye,
and I am labeled
as "teacher's pet."
It's then that I am tempted to listen
to the whispers of the Enemy
telling me that I should really seek employment
somewhere else.

But at the moment, Lord,
you haven't indicated
that I am free to leave this
    place.
So help me to see people
    with your eyes,
and thank you for the
    stories in your Word
that tell us that a
    shepherd's rod can part
    the sea,
a boy can fell a giant with
    one small stone,
and the foundations
of city walls can crumble
when people march in step with one another,
and then proclaim their trust in you
with an almighty shout!5

If you want to enjoy life
and see many happy days,
keep your tongue from speaking evil
and your lips from telling lies.
Turn away from evil and do good.
Search for peace, and work to
    maintain it.
The eyes of the Lord watch over those
    who do right,
and his ears are open to their prayers.

1 PETER 3:10–12 NLT

Why, Lord, Why?

I will instruct you and teach you in the way you should go;
I will counsel you and watch over you.

PSALM 32:8

~

Let's spend less energy trying to read God's
mind on why He does what He does and more
on doing what He wants us to do.

JOYCE MEYER

Dear Lord, I simply do not understand
just what it is
that you are doing in my life.
I thought that I had heard your voice
telling me
that this job was God-given.
And it truly seemed to be
the perfect match for my experience and abilities.

And now, Lord, just as I was settling in
there seems to be a serious chance
that I'll be made redundant.[6]
"Last in, first out" is how my colleagues put it
as they whisper together, eyeing me,

closing ranks,
because they all fear for their own employment.

Dear Lord, whatever way
the management may wrap it up,
I feel I'm much less valued than the rest.
Dispensable, not yet established,
easy to move on.
And yet I left the company where I had worked for years
for this,
thinking that I had been obedient,
responsive to your call.
So did I make a horrible mistake?

My husband tells me not to panic, Lord.
To wait until we know the outcome
of this hard management decision.
For we've seen in the past
that our times are truly in your hands.

Living a life of faith means never knowing where you are being led. But it does mean loving and knowing the One who is leading. It is literally a life of *faith*, not of understanding and reason—a life of knowing Him who calls us to go. Faith is rooted in the knowledge of a Person, and one of the biggest traps we fall into is the belief that if we have faith, God will surely lead us to success in the world.

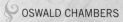 OSWALD CHAMBERS

And if you call us
to step into the dark with you,
you'll neither leave us nor forsake us,
even though
tonight this puzzling situation
 doesn't seem to make the smallest bit of sense.

It isn't necessary to understand in order to obey.
Surrendered people obey God even when it doesn't
seem to make sense. Abraham followed God without
knowing WHERE it would take him. Hannah waited for
God's timing without knowing WHEN. Mary expected
a miracle without knowing HOW. Joseph trusted God's
plan without knowing WHY circumstances happened
as they did. Each was fully surrendered to God and
they came out on top. How will I know that I'm fully
surrendered? When I rely on God to work things out,
instead of trying to manipulate others, force my own
agenda, or control the situation.

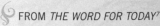 FROM *THE WORD FOR TODAY*[7]

A Woman and Her Family of Faith

The church is a family, full of sinful, broken people experiencing the adventure of life and faith together. We are not part of God's family because we are better than others, but because we have recognized our need and our total inability to change ourselves. Within the sheltering walls of true Christian community, we can know real relationships, and receive healing for our brokenness and supportive accountability as we grow in grace.

 MARION STROUD

The community of faith does not need brilliant personalities but faithful servants of Jesus and of one another. It does not lack the former, but the latter.

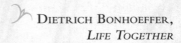 DIETRICH BONHOEFFER,
LIFE TOGETHER

What a Privilege!

I rejoiced with those who said to me,
"Let us go to the house of the Lord."

PSALM 122:1

~

Just as our bodies have many parts and each part has a
special function, so it is with Christ's body. We are many
parts of one body, and we all belong to each other.

ROMANS 12:4–5 NLT

It's such a privilege to be part of your family, Lord,
although sometimes
I don't appreciate it as I should,
and I have been known
to serve "roast preacher" for our lunch
on Sundays.
Forgive me, Lord.
From this day forward
I really want to be more grateful
that you have given me
this wonderful, if random, group of people,
each one a vital member of my family of faith,
and gathered us together to be "church"
in this particular location.

Thank you for our leaders,
who've grasped the challenge
of leading such a varied group of men and women,
teaching us your Word
and helping us to grow up into Christ,[8]
although in many lives this growth
must seem so painstakingly slow.
And sometimes
they must feel as if they're herding cats,
who all seem totally intent in choosing
their own direction.

There are so many different gifts, dear Lord,
with which you've graced
the members of our church.
Thank you for musicians who can lead us
into your presence
and set the scene for worship,
blending the sounds of many instruments
into a heart–inspiring
song of praise.
Thank you for the hours they spend
in practice and in preparation,
something we often take for granted
as we arrive for services each week.

Then, Lord, there are the people
to whom you've given
both the ability and the desire
to teach and pastor.
Thank you for those who teach our children
and provide a safe place for our teens

to share the joys and challenges
of growing up.
Thank you too for those who lead
small groups of adults,
adding the time that's needed
to plan and prepare
to an already busy working life.

We often don't appreciate the people
who use their practical abilities
to keep our building in good order,
set out the chairs each week,
and faithfully ensure
that the rooms in which we gather
are fresh and clean.
Remind me, Lord, to thank them
and to be ready
to play my part in doing these
less glamorous background tasks
essential for the functioning
of our life together.

In every family, dear Lord,
there are occasions
when people don't treat one another
as they should.
Please save our church from factions,
cliques, and times when personalities
become determined
to have their way.

Help me to be a peacemaker
rather than a participant,

especially if the problem stems from people
whom I find hard to get along with.

Your parting words to your disciples, Lord,
were that they should love,
that this would be the hallmark of your church.
And love, it's said,
"Ever gives, forgives, outlives.
And ever stands with open hands
And while it lives
it gives.
For this is love's prerogative—
to give and give and give."[9]
Lord, make me one
who loves you and my "forever family"
like that.

Christ has no body now but yours,
No hands, no feet on earth but yours,
Yours are the eyes with which he looks
Compassion on the world.
Yours are the feet with which he walks to
    do good,
Yours are the hands with which he blesses
all the world.

TERESA OF AVILA

Belonging

~

"The next time you put on a dinner, don't just invite
your friends and family and rich neighbors, the kind
of people who will return the favor. Invite some people
who never get invited out, the misfits from the wrong
side of the tracks. You'll be—and experience—a blessing.
They won't be able to return the favor, but the favor
will be returned—oh, how it will be returned!—at
the resurrection of God's people."
LUKE 14:12–14, THE MESSAGE

Dear God, I need to talk to you
about the "in" crowd.
Wherever women gather—
school gates, the drinking fountain at the gym,
or even here at church—
there'll always be a group that flocks together,
bright eyed and smartly dressed,
laughing at the same jokes, knowing the same people,
praying for one another
with arm flung round a shoulder,
and seemingly protected by a shining wall
    of confidence
that appears impossible for other folk to climb.

At my old church, I would have been there with them.
Leading this, arranging that,
acknowledged, loved, and wanted.
But not here, not now.
Today I slipped in quietly, sat solitary, spoke to no one,
even though my heart was crying,
"I'm here! I want to be your friend."
And when I took my courage in both hands and went for
     coffee,
I drank it in a corner, all alone.

You talked to pig keepers and lepers, Lord.
Each one considered, at the time, untouchable.
And women, who went out to wells at noon,
as well as occupying troops and tax-collecting traitors
were frequently made welcome at your table.
In fact you said that you have special places
reserved, not for the great and good,

Visit the old, the sick, the elderly. Take your
neighbor a new dish . . . Take time to make friends
with individuals who might ordinarily be outside
your social group. The Good Samaritan has lived
in memory for centuries without a name. The best
friends are not always the most important people.
See yourself as a person worthy of love, even if
no one at the moment seems to be tripping over
his feet . . . to tell you so . . . But recognize that
loneliness won't disappear overnight. It may have
to be swept out . . . each day.

KATIE FUNK WIEBE

but for the least and lowest,
for they have always been your friends.

Please put your arm around my shoulder, Lord.
Help me not to take personally
what seems like a rejection.
Keep me from thinking of them critically
and shrinking from them nervously.
Remind me that for all those women
who would consider
that they "belong,"
there are so many others seeking friends.
Like me, just longing for a touch, a word, a smile.
So give me courage to hold out my hand, Lord,
and offer what I can, for you have said
that anything I do for alien or stranger
I do for you.

Mystery Worshipper

~

Don't forget to show hospitality to strangers, for some who have done this have entertained angels without realizing it!

HEBREWS 13:2 NLT

Dear Lord, we had a stranger in our midst
at church last week,
and she was not an ordinary visitor,
but what they call these days
a mystery worshipper.

I've heard of mystery shoppers, Lord,
and even thought that I would like try
to test nearby shops for
stock range and convenience,
and see how many bored assistants
would stand and chat with others,
rather than be alert and ready
to help someone
with limited mobility.
But mystery worshippers sound altogether different.

Apparently what happens
is that somebody from out of town,
and not familiar with our church,
pays us a visit unannounced.

They look at church facilities,
from parking lot to the nursery.
They rate us on our warmth of welcome,
style of service,
and even
the length and helpfulness
of what is preached.
And then they send the pastor a report,
so we can see ourselves as others see us.

Some people are quite angry, Lord,
and feel that we've been spied upon
and treated quite unfairly.
But surely it is better to know
that people find our parking lot
both cramped and dangerous
because we don't have volunteers
directing traffic
and children run around
without a thought of danger
from moving vehicles.

We got good marks for the enthusiasm
of those who lead our worship,
but I must agree that it is hard
to hear their voices
above the noise of drums
amplified at full volume.

Our mystery worshipper
was welcomed at the door, she said,
but no one thought to show her

the hall that held the children's classes,
and during coffee
most people seemed too occupied
to talk to her.

It's made me think, dear Lord,
and analyze my own behavior.
I must confess
that I'm not quick to welcome strangers,
especially if they're from another nation,
because I worry that I may not understand their accent
or won't be able to pronounce their name.

And now I really blush to think
that when I find the seat in which I often sit
is occupied,
I have been known to look a little frosty.
But now it horrifies me to think
that I could be complaining
about an angel.

So thank you, Lord, for mystery worshippers.
Now give us grace and real determination
to make our church,
both building and its people,
the best that it can be.
And to remember
that we're your representatives
and we're responsible
to give an accurate account
of who you are
and what you have to offer
to all who seek you.

As It Was at the Beginning

Ascribe to the Lord the glory due his name;
bring an offering and come into his courts.
Worship the Lord in the splendor of his holiness;
tremble before him, all the earth.

PSALM 96:8–9

~

"Our Father in heaven, hallowed be your name, your
kingdom come, your will be done on earth as it is in heaven."

MATTHEW 6:9–10

~

We do not wish anything to happen.
Seven years have we lived quietly,
Succeeded in avoiding notice,
Living and partly living.

T. S. ELIOT, MURDER IN THE CATHEDRAL

It's Sunday, Lord,
a day to which I usually look forward.
But now I go to worship with a heavy heart.
For, Lord, you know about the cloud
that looms so large and dark on our horizon
and threatens

to tear apart the very fabric of our lives,
unless we find a godly resolution
to all the problems that we face at church.

In many ways this challenge is a good thing, Lord.
It is the fruit of life and growth,
not staleness and decay.
You would have thought that those of us
who've worshipped here for
      many years
would be so pleased about the
      way the church has grown
that we'd be ready to support
more services, a bigger building,
fresh styles of music,
and a new approach to reaching
      our community.
You would expect
that we would joyfully make room
for all the challenges that baby Christians bring.

> Many people are in a rut, and
> a rut is nothing but a grave—
> with both ends kicked out.
>
> VANCE HAVNER

Instead of that, dear Lord,
we seem to have been driven into factions.
So those who welcome change,
and want to move in tune
with what appear to be the wind words of your spirit,
are bitterly opposed
by those who like the old ways,
prefer the services we've always had,
reject the plans to make more space,
and grieve at the thought of change
and sailing out into uncharted waters.

Please help us, Lord.
Give wisdom to our leaders,
and then a readiness in each of us to put aside
our preferences,
the little things that in our day
were good and right,
but now just hinder and impede your work.
Help us to make these necessary changes
with grace and kindness,
while understanding what belongs
to the foundations of our faith
and what is window dressing.
And please, Lord, keep us very much aware
of which is which.

For in the last analysis
    we need to grasp
that it is you we come to
    worship,
and when we bring our
    praises and petitions to
    your throne,
the "how" is not the
    issue,
for you can see our
    hearts.

> "If you are offering your gift at the altar and there remember that your brother has something against you, leave your gift there in front of the altar. First go and be reconciled to your brother; then come and offer your gift."
>
> MATTHEW 5:23–24

You know if it is love of you and neighbor
that shapes our words and actions.
Help us to turn to you
with reverence and awe,
to give and to receive the gentle touch
of your forgiveness.

And then when you say "come," dear Lord,
help us to fix our eyes on you,
stepping out, with neither "murmurings,
nor disputings,"[10]
to follow you with joy,
wherever you may lead.

> In vain I have searched the Bible, looking for
> examples of early Christians whose lives were marked
> by rigidity, predictability, inhibition, dullness, and
> caution. Fortunately, grim, frowning, joyless saints in
> Scripture are conspicuous by their absence. Instead,
> the examples I find are of adventurous, risk-taking,
> enthusiastic, and authentic believers whose joy was
> contagious even in times of painful trial. Their vision
> was broad even when death drew near.
>
> CHUCK SWINDOLL

Boundaries

"Suppose one of you wants to build a tower. Will he not first sit down and estimate the cost to see if he has enough money to complete it? For if he lays the foundation and is not able to finish it, everyone who sees it will ridicule him, saying, 'This fellow began to build and is not able to finish.'"

LUKE 14:28–30

~

Very early in the morning, while it was still dark, Jesus got up, left the house and went off to a solitary place, where he prayed. Simon and his companions went to look for him, and when they had found him, they exclaimed: "Everyone is looking for you!" Jesus replied "Let us go somewhere else—to the nearby villages—so I can preach there also. That is why I have come."

MARK 1:35–38

Dear Lord, what have I done?
Well, that's a silly question really,
because I've made the same mistake
so many times before.
You know the one.
People ask me if I'd like to help
with this or that activity at church,
and I don't wait to think about the implications

of yet another regular commitment
and merrily say yes, then panic later.

Of course it's good to be available.
But it is also true
that the same few volunteers
seem to bear
the heavy burden of responsibility
for everything that's deemed to be
beyond the job of those who serve the church full-time.

And there's a subtle pressure, Lord,
rooted in the well-intentioned phrase
we learned in Sunday school,
where we were told that if we want to
    know true joy,
we need to put Jesus first,
others next, and ourselves last of all.
Is that how you want us to live, dear Lord?
When overload of church commitments can result
in homes and families neglected,
and frantic, frazzled women
who certainly do not reflect your peace and joy,
or your serenity.

My husband points me to the times, dear Lord,
when you withdrew for prayer,
or did not let hyped-up disciples
dictate to whom you spoke
or what you did
when pressed upon by anxious crowds.
You had a clear view of your boundaries:

Here to do your Father's will, and nothing else.
Why can't I be like you?

Sometimes I wish that someone else
would make it clear
what tasks I should or shouldn't volunteer for.
But in my saner moments,
I know that I can get that guidance
only when I give quiet attention
to what you've gifted me to do.
Then I must make clear,
both to myself and others,
the boundaries I need to put in place.

You know that I've attempted
to do that very thing at other times,
and then before long found myself
sabotaging my decisions
because I am afraid of seeming lazy,
losing friendships,
or missing out on something interesting and fun.
Or because, for some odd reason,
I'm absolutely
unable to say no.

Please help me, Lord.
Help me to recognize that, as the psalmist said,
"You have assigned me my portion and my cup,"
and in doing so "have made my lot secure."
I praise you, Lord, for it is true
"The boundary lines have fallen
for me in pleasant places;

surely I have a delightful inheritance."[11]
Help me to be content
with those things you have planned for me to do
and confident enough in you
to say no, kindly and politely,
when people
try to lead me into other things.

A Christmas Prayer

*Take time to be aware that in the very midst of our
busy preparations for the celebration of Christ's birth
in ancient Bethlehem, Christ is reborn in the Bethlehems
of our homes and daily lives. Take time, slow down, be
still, be awake to the Divine Mystery that looks so
common and so ordinary yet is wondrously present.*

EDWARD HAYS

~

Christmas, my child, is love in action.

DALE EVANS ROGERS

Dear Lord,
you know I long to celebrate your birth
in ways that bring you joy.
And yet it is so very hard
when others in my family
see this time of year as nothing
but an excuse for far too much of everything,
except the one to whom the festival belongs.

Please help me, Lord.
If I can't be at church to celebrate
within the family of faith,
show me a way to bring to you my worship,

even if the most that I can do
is simply to stretch out my hand
with loving reverence
amidst the hurly-burly
of our December days.

Sometimes, dear Lord, it seems
our present-giving customs
are threatening to spoil this time of year.
Please help me to spend our limited resources
wisely, thankfully,
thoughtfully—
praising you for what I have
and ways in which I can bring others joy
instead of mourning
the things that I may lack.

The final gift
the magi laid low at your feet, dear Lord,
was myrrh,
which spoke of suffering
and pain that lay ahead.[12]
My little sadnesses are nothing
compared with that.

So when I feel alone,
misunderstood,
or simply tired,
help me remember
that I can offer all my days
and bring you joy
by gift-wrapping them

in jewel-bright colors of your Spirit's fruit
and labeling them
"All for Jesus,
with love,
from me."

Just Another Man?

Two are better than one . . .
If one falls down, his friend can help him up.
But pity the man who falls and has no one to help him up!

. . .

Though one may be overpowered,
two can defend themselves.
A cord of three strands is not quickly broken.

ECCLESIASTES 4:9–12

~

As long as Moses held up the staff in his hand, the Israelites
had the advantage. But . . . Moses' arms soon became so tired
he could no longer hold them up. So Aaron and Hur . . .
stood on each side of Moses, holding up his hands.

EXODUS 17:11–12 NLT

It's all across the media, Lord.
A pastor,
well known throughout the area,
apparently successful and sold out for you,
has found the weight of leadership
impossible to shoulder any longer
and has shot himself.

He's left his wife and children utterly bereft,
his congregation spilt right down the middle,

and people pointing fingers at the church again,
saying, "You never see smoke without a fire"
and whispering,
"Whatever was he up to?
He must have been deeply into sin
if he should feel
so utterly consumed by pain
that he could see no other option
than to take this very permanent way out."

They say he left a note, dear Lord.
"I can't hold this together anymore" was all it said.
But in those six short words,
we read so much of what was going on
within his church and congregation.
For some of his parishioners
had fallen out
with others in the church,
and in the warfare that had raged
between the groups,
it was their leader who'd become the casualty.

In trying to promote your standards, Lord,
of peace and reconciliation,
he had become the victim,
pleasing neither side,
and finally becoming
the object of their wrath.

Dear Lord, why do we ask,
indeed demand,
impossible perfection
from those who lead your church?

For we so often think that they should be
a cross between the angel Gabriel
and business gurus like Bill Gates.

In smaller congregations it's expected
that he can do it all—
preach and pastor,
innovate and swing the door wide open
to people who have never been to church,
without offending
those who have been there for many years.
And when the numbers grow and he becomes
a leader of a team of men and women,
we think that he should have the gifts
it takes to run a good-sized corporation,
although his training in no way qualified him
to undertake a major task like that.

I have to ask myself if I am guilty
of secretly expecting those who lead the church
to be all things to men,
and, yes, to women, Lord.
Do I expect them to be ready
to answer all my questions about belief
and biblical interpretation,
to be available to me at any time
both day and night,
for "after all, we're paying them"
and "Sunday is their only busy day!"

And if their children
should cross the line in any way
from what has been

traditionally expected of "preacher's kids,"
our criticism knows no bounds,
and we make no allowance for the fact
that they're just kids like any others.
If only we would turn our close attention
back to ourselves,
we'd see so many failings
in our family and parenting
that we would have to hang our heads in shame
and pray for them
as we pray for ourselves.

Forgive us, Lord,
and help us in the future
to walk a few miles in their shoes
before we grumble and complain.
Help those who share these leadership responsibilities
to love and to support each other
and to trust, so that they can share

"Do not judge, or you too will be judged. For in the same way you judge others, you will be judged, and with the measure you use, it will be measured to you . . . How can you say to your brother, 'Let me take the speck out of your eye,' when all the time there is a plank in your own eye? You hypocrite, first take the plank out of your own eye, and then you will see clearly to remove the speck from your brother's eye."

MATTHEW 7:1–5

their fears, their problems, and their weaknesses
without the fear of condemnation
from those who serve beside them.

And most of all, Lord, help them
to know the shelter of your loving arms,
protecting them
from all that Satan sends their way.
And may I never be part of a problem
that causes any Christian leader
to fall aside
because they cannot hold their life together
anymore.

A Woman and the Wider World

We hear your call to go—go and make disciples,
identify with strangers, walk on shifting sands, and
  build a kingdom church.
"Go" is not a comfortable word.
Teach us how to depend on you again;
we need your initiative, your boldness, your blessing,
  your plan.
Make us unafraid to break new ground,
to take new faith steps with you.
Do a new thing, Father . . .
Give a new passion for worship, a new love
  for the lost,
a new unity in purpose, a new strength in our resolve,
a new heart of repentance, a new humanity of spirit,
a new pulse for the people, a new heart laid bare,
and send us out.

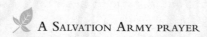 **A Salvation Army prayer**

The Enemy Within

~

Do not be idolators, as some of them were . . .
We should not commit sexual
immorality, as some of them did . . .
We should not test the Lord, as some of them did . . .
And do not grumble, as some of them did . . .
No temptation has seized you except what is
common to man. And God is faithful; he will not let
you be tempted beyond what you can bear. But when
you are tempted, he will also provide a way out so
that you can stand up under it.

1 CORINTHIANS 10:7–13

I said I wouldn't do it anymore, Lord.
I promised that I'd stay within my spending limit,
keep away from window-shopping,
and only visit stores
if I was making a particular purchase,
which both of us agreed was necessary
for me to buy right now.

But Lord, the statement for my credit card
reveals the truth.
I had forgotten
that gloomy day last month

when everything was going wrong
and I just had to leave the office
and fill my lunch hour
with something that would cheer me up.

I didn't mean to shop, dear Lord,
but when it rains, the mall is
the only dry place that's available.
You know that I intended
to get some lunch,
walk briskly up and down,
and then go back to the office.
But when I saw
my favorite store was running
a twenty-four-hour sale,
it seemed quite foolish to ignore
the bargains to be had.

Right there before my eyes were
so many items that could so easily be used
as Christmas presents.
In fact it seemed quite irresponsible
not to take
advantage of the situation.
But now I have to pay.

And Lord, if I'm completely honest,
it isn't just the shopping malls
that sing to me with siren voices.
Last week there was the evening spent online
where everything was so available,
and just one click
secured a huge variety of things.

The auction sites like eBay
had their own fascination
until my husband
found me creeping down to my computer,
although it was the middle of the night,
because I felt
compelled to see if I'd secured
the item on which I had placed a bid.

And now, dear Lord, there are the shopping channels,
which my friend recommended.
So wonderfully available
and fun to watch.
That's all I meant to do,
but somehow, Lord, I simply couldn't sit there
without a tiny step
into that glittering world,
so brightly lit, just like Aladdin's cave.

I really do not understand it, Lord.
Why do I try to fill that emptiness inside
with things when I feel sad,
or when hormones roar round my body?
Whatever's at the root of this,
I can't excuse it any longer.
I cannot keep on spending money
that we do not have.

Your Word has promised that you'll lead me
to a way out.
I know I'm not the only one to struggle in this way,
but here and now

I must confess that I am powerless
to deal with this myself.
I have done all I can to break free
of this compulsion,
and things aren't getting any better.

So please, Lord, take this problem
and nail it to your cross.
I don't know what you'll do to change me,
but I do know you love me
and want the best for me.
So please, Lord, let your Spirit fill my heart
and show me what to do.

Have You Given Some Thought to Your Food?

~

Then the King will say to those on his right, "Come,
you who are blessed by my Father; take your inheritance,
the kingdom prepared for you since the creation of the
world". . . Then the righteous will answer him, "Lord,
when did we see you hungry and feed you, or thirsty and
give you something to drink?" . . . The King will reply,
"I tell you the truth, whatever you did for one of the least
of these brothers of mine, you did for me."

MATTHEW 25:34–40

Charity begins at home, dear Lord,
or that is what we say
when economic times are hard
and we are looking for a refuge
from constant calls upon our purse.
And I yet can't forget him,
that little child
 with fly-blown eyes and swollen stomach,
standing there in line
waiting, exhausted,
for just one cupful of the precious rice
that will provide his only meal
today.

He's three years old and yet he's walked
for four long weeks
to reach a place where there's a kind of safety,
even though his home's a canvas shelter,
and he depends on others
for gifts of food.

How can his parents bear it, Lord?
To see crops fail and children whom they love,
in every way as I love mine,
cry out from hunger,
while they are very well aware
 that if there is no rain
and no seed left to plant for next year's harvest,
the very best that they can hope for
is aid from nations far away.

What would he think about my
    laden cart,
that little boy who must survive
on one small meal a day?
We eat so much in one short
    week.
And we are on a budget, Lord.
There is no money for luxuries.
I have to buy
the bargains and the special
    offers.
I can't afford to give to others
    . . . or can I?

If I just bought two items
for which the grower would be paid

Though I am surrounded by
    troubles . . .
the Lord will work out his plans
    for my life—
for your faithful love,
O Lord, endures forever.

 PSALM 138:7–8 NLT

a living wage,
or used coupons
to buy an extra can or two of food
to give to those
who will depend this week on food
    banks
right here within my city,
 putting aside
some of the junk food that we love,
would it really make a difference?

Thank you for reminding me today, Lord,
 that as just one person
 I can't change the world,
but I can still make a difference for one person.
Somebody's life and dignity
may well depend
upon the items I take from supermarket shelves,
put in my shopping cart,
and spread before my family.

Help me to shop with others' needs in mind,
and as I do so,
give me a thankful heart
 for all that others do for me.
Remind me, Lord, that no one is an island,
and all that you require of me
is that I act justly,
 in this and other areas of my life,
with joy and thankfulness.

Do all the good you can,
By all the means you can,
In all the ways you can,
In all the places you can,
At all the times you can,
To all the people you can,
As long as ever you can.

JOHN WESLEY

Man Down!

*"Greater love has no one than this, that
he lay down his life for his friends."*

JOHN 15:13

~

How the mighty fallen in battle!
Jonathan lies slain on your heights.
I grieve for you, Jonathan my brother;
you were very dear to me.
Your love for me was wonderful,
more wonderful than that of women.

2 SAMUEL 1:25–26

"Man down!" That's what they shout, Lord,
when one of those they call "comrades in arms"
sprawls wounded on the desert sand,
or, worst of all, lies dead.
And this man was so young, dear Lord,
just three days short of twenty-one.
Now he'll have no use for gift-wrapped packages
so neatly stowed beneath his army bunk.

"Always laughing," his teacher said of him.
"He brought the sun inside with him
and made our school a better place."

And that is what he sought to do that day, Lord—
to make the world a better place.
Even when his world was now a sun-baked gully
in a foreign land.

In ambush, snipers watched and waited
while he, and many like him,
searched for and then disarmed
those lethal IEDs.
He made the sandy path a little safer
for those who came behind,
hoping that by his skill and courage,
he would to prevent
another agonizing shout of "man down."

You know about self-sacrifice, dear Lord.
For "greater love," you said while here on earth,
has no one showed than this:
that one may lay down his life for his friends.[13]
And that is what you did.

No bombs or bullets took your
    life.
Knowing very well what lie
    ahead
and sweating blood, you chose
the whip, the thorns, the spittle,
    and the taunts,
and for your enemies,
as well as for your friends,
you chose the nails.

Let us fix our eyes on Jesus, the author and perfecter of our faith, who for the joy set before him endured the cross, scorning its shame . . . Consider him who endured such opposition from sinful men, so that you will not grow weary and lose heart.

HEBREWS 12:2–3

And now, Lord, you have called each one of us
to fight against the enemy of souls.
Not flesh and blood,
but rulers, powers, and evil spiritual forces
in unseen realms.
Not visible, but prowling nonetheless
to weaken and destroy.

Today please help us to stand,
arms linked,
strong in your power,
protected by your blood,
so that whatever stratagem the enemy employs,
the shout will not go up for us,
"Man down!"

The Suitcase

The two disciples . . . followed Jesus . . .
They said, "Rabbi . . . where are you staying?"
"Come," he replied, "and you will see."
So they went and saw where he was
staying, and spent that day with him.

JOHN 1:37–39

~

Why is it that so many Muslims and Hindus and
Buddhists (85 percent [living in our country], to be
somewhat precise) do not have a personal relationship
with a Christian? . . . Somehow I doubt it is the fault
of most of those Muslims, Hindus, and Buddhists.

JUSTIN LONG

~

An Englishman's home is his castle.

ENGLISH PROVERB

He left behind a suitcase full of gifts, Lord.
Gifts that he had brought with him
to share with those who gave him hospitality,
for in his country it would be unthinkable
to see a stranger
and not invite him into your home.

This student lived among us
for four long years,
and no one offered him
a chance to understand what Easter signifies,
a meal at Thanksgiving,
or a bed at Christmas.
Truly, for this young man,
so far from family and his own culture,
there was no room in our particular inn.

Why is it, Lord,
that we are so reluctant
to open up our homes to those from other lands?
In fact, if we are honest,
we rarely entertain at all,
unless it's family,
or people we have known for years.

Of course we're quick to conjure up excuses.
We're too busy,
our homes too small, too shabby,
or not comfortable enough
for visitors.
We say we don't know what we'd do
to entertain a guest
whose English might be poor,
who might not like our food or customs,
when really if we're honest,
we do not want to make the effort
to obey your command
to be hospitable to strangers.

Dear Lord, forgive us.
For we spend many hours at church
praying fervently
for missionaries in foreign lands,
but then ignore
the many, many members of another faith
who study in our cities.
They may go home
without the opportunity
to hear about your love.

Please help me, Lord.
I don't have much in common
with these young people who are far from home.
But if you'll open a way for me to meet them,
and give me courage to stretch out my hand,
then when they ask, as the disciples did,
"Where do you live?"
I'll lower that creaking drawbridge,
and with a smile I'll answer
"Come and see."

We spend a lot of time reaching out to the rich, the famous,
the cool, the successful, the powerful, the influential, the
ones with the right style of glasses. I could be wrong, but
it seems to me Jesus didn't spend a whole lot of time with
people who rejected Him. He didn't spend years trying
to persuade them. So why is it we spend years trying to
persuade the stubbornly, rebelliously atheistic cousin (or
nephew or uncle or whatever) and never reach out to the
foreign exchange student?

 JUSTIN LONG

Looking on the Outside

Dear Lord, why is it
that I have this awful tendency
to judge both things and people
from the way that they appear
on the outside?

The latest victim of my criticizing heart
was that unusual woman
I met while on vacation,
with purple hair

and wearing clothes
that seemed so totally unsuitable
for climate and conditions.

She grumbled and found fault with everything
until we all avoided
sharing her table,
sitting near her,
or speaking to her at all, if we could help it.

And yet, Lord, when I finally
plucked up the courage
to walk a little way with her,
I learned that her name is Aimee Rose,
which means "beloved" or "loved one."

Once upon a time somebody loved her,
welcomed her
into the world with joy,
and gave her names
that spoke of someone to be treasured.

I wonder what went wrong?
What pain and loss has touched her life
so that she marches through her days
aggressive
and isolated from normal human contact,
repelling others by her attitude,
yet desperately needing
to be loved and accepted once again.

Please help me, Lord.
Give me your eyes and ears

and set me free from prejudice,
assessing others
by the color of their skin,
their clothes, their education, or their accent.

Help me to live quite unimpressed
by things that others own or lack,
remembering that while on earth,
you moved among the prostitutes
and men of power and influence
with equal ease.
Remind me too that whatever name
our parents may have given us,
to you we are all Aimee,
"the loved one."

The Lord said to Samuel, ". . . Fill your horn with oil . . . I am sending you to Jesse of Bethlehem. I have chosen one of his sons to be king." . . . When they arrived, Samuel saw Eliab and thought, "Surely the Lord's anointed stands here before the Lord." But the Lord said to Samuel, "Do not consider his appearance or his height, for I have rejected him. The Lord does not look at the things man looks at. Man looks at the outward appearance, but the Lord looks at the heart."

1 SAMUEL 16:1–7

The Return

It took at least six months to adjust. I cried a lot.
You need to be very strong before you return.

A RETURNEE

~

There are two different programs in me. I feel
as if I'm a foreigner in my own country.

A RETURNEE

She's going home, Lord.
And in a way, that is a matter for rejoicing.
She has finished
her further education
and returns to China
with an advanced degree
and three years' experience
of living in the West.
Best of all, she has discovered
that you're alive and active,
and want to be her friend.

But when I think about her future,
I'm sometimes tempted
to fear for her.
It seems her family is displeased
about the change in her religion,

and she knows no one else who shares her faith
"back home."
She has no idea if there's a Christian church
where she'll be living.
In these and in so many other ways,
dear Lord, we have to face the fact
that her faith is likely
to be severely tested.

Please help us, Lord,
to do the very best we can
to thoroughly prepare her
for her "reentry,"
as it is called.
It sounds a bit like coming back from space,
but I guess that seeing her old life
through Christian eyes
is likely to be almost as strange
as for an astronaut
returning to earth.
Because in many, many ways,
she is a different person.

Please give her friends.
Point us to people who can connect her
with other Chinese graduates
who've followed her faith journey.
It seems that it is not as simple for her
as just finding any church.
For she will have to learn
a different style of Chinese worship,
and other ways of "doing church,"

which are unlikely to be the same
as those she has experienced here,
for all that she has known so far
is Western Christianity.

Then there are customs
like worshipping the ancestors
of which she can no longer be a part.
And she longs to find
   a husband
who will share her
   faith
but that is hardly
   likely
if her parents handle
   the arrangements.
How will she cope if
   parents
still demand
the same compliance
   to their wishes
in everything—
matters of faith included?
Oh help her, Lord, to know
what parts of Chinese culture
are appropriate for someone
whose faith is based upon the Bible.

> The Lord now chose seventy-two other disciples and sent them ahead in pairs to all the towns and places he planned to visit. These were his instructions to them: "The harvest is great, but the workers are few . . . Now go, and remember that I am sending you out as lambs among wolves."
>
> LUKE 10:1–3 NLT

Dear Lord, I'm thankful you have promised
that you'll be with your followers every day,
no matter where life takes us,
and you'll provide all that we need.

Thank you that she values
everything she now knows of you,
and that she has said
it will be worth whatever price
she has to pay in order to remain
your faithful child.

Lord, I'm not sure I could be
just as courageous.
And maybe there will be some days
when she is tempted to turn back.
Please hold her close, Lord,
and as she takes your light to that vast land
where you're not known in many places,
please use her to teach others
and so expand your kingdom.

Something Beautiful for God?

~

While Jesus was in Bethany . . . a woman came to
him with an alabaster jar of very expensive perfume, which
she poured on his head as he was reclining at the table.
When the disciples saw this, they were indignant. "Why
this waste?" they asked. "This perfume could have been sold
at a high price and the money given to the poor." Aware
of this, Jesus said to them, "Why are you bothering this
woman? She has done a beautiful thing to me."

MATTHEW 26:6–10

She sat within the doorway of that little church
muffled in gloves and scarf.
Her shabby winter coat was barely thick enough
to keep her warm.
And yet she stayed there in the early morning chill
pulling the rope that reached the bell tower,
so that the single bell tolled out its message,
"The church is here;
God is waiting.
Come and worship."

The building has survived, dear Lord,
through the years

when atheistic forces ruled the land.
But now, perhaps God seems irrelevant,
and church attendance
is deemed both dull and out-of-date
by those who've never known you.
For though I watched her for at least an hour,
as far as I could tell from where I sat,
warm and cozy in my comfortable hotel,
no one came.

Did her arms ache, dear Lord,
and was her heart discouraged?
Feeling perhaps
that it was hardly worth enduring
the cold, the early rising,
the tuneless clanging
of that solitary bell,
when no one came?

For, Lord, you couldn't say it was a lovely sound.
Unlike the joyous peals
that thunder out
from churches and cathedrals,
created by a team of eager "campanologists,"
the sound a thing of beauty in and of itself,
this tuneless bell
brought no one to the church
in her small village,
and little seemed to happen
to reward her work.

And yet, Lord,
when you whispered to my heart,

"You don't see what is going on
within the hearts of those who hear,"
I realized
that at the very least
she had an audience
of two.
You, Lord, who saw her sacrifice of love
and treasured it.
And me,
to whom you spoke so clearly.

So thank you, Lord,
for all the people
who faithfully rise early
and labor late,
doing the little things you've asked of them,
in spite of difficulties and disappointments,
"tolling" their particular bell
so that the people all around them,
whether they seem to listen and respond
or not,
can know that God is here.

These people day by day repeat the news
that you both love and value everyone
and wait with arms outstretched
for them to find their way back home,
to worship.

It's Not Our Business

"A man was going down from Jerusalem to Jericho, when
he fell into the hands of robbers. They . . . beat him and
went away, leaving him half dead . . . When [a priest]
saw the man, he passed by on the other side. So too, a Levite
. . . But a Samaritan . . . came where the man was;
and when he saw him, he took pity on him.

LUKE 10:30–33

~

The greatest sins of our time are committed not by the few
who have destroyed, but by the vast majority who sat idly by.

MARTIN LUTHER KING JR.

We do it all too often, Lord.
We see a wrong in our society
and may feel most indignant at the time.
We really do intend to write that letter
of protest
to the media,
set up a system to recycle
the rubbish we produce,
or take a step to remedy
that clear example of injustice . . .
but somehow we don't rouse ourselves

from our inertia,
and nothing changes.

Sometimes the issues are more hidden, Lord,
and to expose them
might put our reputation,
our credibility,
or even our employment
on the line.
The temptation that assails us then, dear Lord,
is to ignore the deep uneasiness we feel,
not wanting to be called a "whistle-blower,"
avoiding the issue until the whole mess
comes to public notice,
and people are amazed.

We try to justify our reticence to get involved.
We say big corporations
can well afford the loss,
and this is basically
a crime without a victim.
What lies we tell ourselves!

And worse, dear Lord,
is when the victims are the helpless ones,
the bullied and the alien,
the children who live lives of quiet desperation,
day-by-day enduring horrors
in mind or body,
while adults
who should protect and keep them safe,
do nothing,
or worst of all perpetuate the wickedness.

How will we stand before you
and make excuses,
knowing you said that
little ones
are so important to
you,
that those who would
molest them or ill–
treat them
would face the wrath
of an all–seeing
God?
Yet we align ourselves
with wicked people
by keeping silent.

Oh help us, Lord.
We are your people,
and your Word tells us
that you require us
to stand against injustice,
whatever shape it takes.

Please free us from the prison of indifference.
Destroy our fear of looking foolish
or of falling out with friends,
or those whose good opinion
has always been important to us.
For in the end, it's only your opinion
that really matters
in time and in eternity.

"This is the kind of fasting I want:
Free those who are wrongfully imprisoned;
lighten the burden of those who work for
you.
Let the oppressed go free,
and remove the chains that bind people.
Share your food with the hungry,
and give shelter to the homeless.
Give clothes to those who need them,
and do not hide from relatives who need
your help."

ISAIAH 58:6–7 NLT

Sunlight and Shadows

The Lord is my shepherd, I shall not be in want.
He makes me lie down in green pastures,
he leads me beside quiet waters,
he restores my soul.

PSALM 23:1–3

~

Give all your worries and cares to
God, for he cares about you.

1 PETER 5:7 NLT

Dear Lord, as I look out upon the world today,
it almost seems uncaring
not to worry.
Even now, my husband has the awful job
of telling people who have worked with him
    for years
that they're redundant.

Good people, who bring hope and loving care
to those dependent on this charity for help.
But now there is no money left to pay the bills
or to support their salaries, and so
not only will the staff be driven out
into the painful wilderness of unemployment,

but those with whom they worked
will be deprived of listening ears and
practical assistance.

Of course they aren't the only people, Lord.
I hardly dare to watch the television news
it is so full of darkness and despair.
Civil war, uprisings in the Middle East—
the news makes
life seem cheap
and death an everyday occurrence.

Starving children fill our screens with hollow eyes,
haunting our hearts with plaintive cries
that are almost beyond their strength to utter.
While in our land, alcohol and drugs
are seen as normal playthings of the young.
Oh help us, Lord.

Where we can make a difference with
    our prayers and giving,
then make us strong and utterly determined
to do the very best we can
to change the situation.
And where it is beyond our scope,
help us to trust you for ourselves and them,
to roll our cares and sadness at your feet
and having done it,
focus on your promises
and all the good things that are ours.

So thank you, Lord, for sunny days.
For healthy babies born

and family reunions.
And we're excited
that in another month a needy child
will be adopted,
finding within our daughter's home
the love and the security
that is her birthright.

I'm grateful, Lord, that there are many
who'll daily work for peace and justice.
Please bless them.
And I rejoice that there are teens
who are investing
some of their precious school-free weeks
in helping others.

Thank you that our fields and gardens
will produce a harvest,
tokens of your ability
to meet our every need,
and thank you that in
    my life
there is more sun than
    shade.
When I see things that
    trouble me,
let me remember
that one day we will see
    all things set right
by you.
Until that great day
    comes, dear Lord,

"That is why I tell you not to worry about everyday life—whether you have enough food and drink, or enough clothes to wear . . . Can all your worries add a single moment to your life? . . . Seek the Kingdom of God above all else, and live righteously, and he will give you everything you need."

MATTHEW 6:25–27, 33 NLT

help me today and every day
to lay my fears and heartaches at your cross,
exchanging them
for peace that passes understanding.

Have you noticed this? Whatever need or trouble
you are in, there is always something to help
you in your Bible, if only you go on reading till
you come to the word God specially has for you.
I have noticed this often. Sometimes the special
word is in the portion you would naturally read,
or in the psalms for the day . . . but you must
go on till you find it, for it is always somewhere.
You will know it the moment you come to it, and
it will rest your heart.

AMY CARMICHAEL

A Woman Growing Older

*Trust me—I gave my life for you because you are so precious
to me. You trusted me at the beginning of your spiritual
journey; trust me now. Nothing is beyond my power.*

*Trust me—I love you and I love those you love more than
you will ever understand. You always have been and
always will be my beloved.*

*Trust me—I can carry you and yours. I long for you to
lean on me with the utter restfulness and assurance of a
sleeping child.*

*Trust me—I am your shepherd and I will lead you in the
right paths. I will see to it that you lack nothing that is
good for you to have.*

*Trust me—even when you can't understand my dealings
with you. Don't give a moment's thought to turning back.*

 **MARION STROUD**

Roots and Wings

*If a widow has children or grandchildren, these should
learn first of all to put their religion into practice by caring
for their own family . . . for this is pleasing to God.*

1 TIMOTHY 5:4

~

*O Jesus, I know well
that You do not look so much
at the greatness of my actions,
as at the love with which I do them.
It is true I am not always faithful,
but I shall not lose courage.
I desire to use every opportunity to please You.*

ST. THERESE OF LISIEUX

Dear Lord, the time has come
for us to offer care to one
who can no longer manage on her own.
You know, Lord,
that she has no desire
to leave the safe familiarity
that she calls home.
But she has fallen several times,
and the activities of daily living

are now a burden,
rather than a joy.

This sharing of our daily lives will be a new experience
for the whole family, Lord,
and each of us will have to make adjustments.
Please help us.
When little ones are born
we often say
that there are two things we need to offer
as they grow up,
"roots" and "wings."
I think perhaps that in this situation,
"roots and wings" are also needed.
So give us wisdom, Lord,
as we seek to provide them.

First she needs to feel secure and welcome,
surrounded by her own familiar things
and rooted in her own routine
as far as we can possibly arrange it.
Thank you that we have the space
to offer her a room,
which she can furnish as she chooses,
and that she won't be moving far away
from friends at church.
Help us to welcome them and be available
to offer lifts where lifts are needed,
so that she can maintain some semblance
of her familiar social life.

Lord, you know that there will be
a balance needed

between the time she spends
within the bosom of the family
and the time she'll spend alone,
for we'll need space to give our children
our time and our attention.
Help us to teach them to respect their Granny,
and to enjoy the special things that she can offer.
Tales of long ago and family history
can help us all to put our roots down firmly
into the stories of your love and care for us
throughout the generations.

The thought of "wings" is not so easy, Lord,
for there is not a great deal she can do.
But give me patience, please,
so if she offers
to help with housework,
or do the mealtime preparations
that fall within her scope,
I will say yes and "that would be a great help,"
even if it would be quicker
to do it all myself.

Lord, you know that I am nervous
about this task I've undertaken
with love, Lord, yes,
but also with a clear awareness
of my own fallibility.
What will happen if I cannot cope, Lord,
or if I lose my patience and regret
the road that we have chosen?
Oh help me, Lord.

Please give me wisdom
when I must make decisions,
compassion and an understanding heart
to recognize her pain and sense of loss,
and patience
so that I act in your time and not my own.

Help me to see my loss of freedom
as a small offering
that I can make to you,
and give me courage so that I can face my fears,
accepting that this is an enormous step
for her as well.
Then give me hope, dear Lord,
so that I'll trust and rest in peace,
believing that as we lean on you,
you will make all things well.

Meister Eckhart once said,
"If the only prayer you say
in your whole life is 'thank you,'
that would suffice."
And so, Lord,
for all that has been,
for all that is,
and for whatever is to come,
I say "thank you."

The Crowning Years

We are filled with the good things of your house.
PSALM 65:4

~

You brought us to a place of abundance.
PSALM 66:12

~

Even the hard pathways overflow with abundance.
The grasslands of the wilderness become a lush pasture,
and the hillsides blossom . . .
They all shout and sing for joy!
PSALM 65:11–13 NLT

~

When morning dawns and evening
fades you call forth songs of joy.
PSALM 65:8

Dear Lord, tomorrow is the day
that I have wished a million miles away,
when I will step, unwillingly,
into a new decade.
Why is it that these days,
these birthdays with a zero in them,

so often seem endowed
with such uncomfortable significance?

For in a world
where youth is everything,
the very fact of getting older, slower,
perhaps less able and less useful
brings with it fear
and thoughts of lack and loss,
instead of celebration for another year well lived.

Oh change my heart, Lord.
Help me view the road that I have walked thus far
with thankfulness.
For you have blessed my life
and done amazing things for me
that filled my heart with joy.
When I have failed,
your grace was always present,
and there have been no darkened valleys
I have had to walk alone.

And now I'm facing
this year of Jubilee,
when in your Word,
outstanding debts were cancelled,
relationships restored,
and slaves set free.
Please help me to grasp hold of life again
intent on making
tomorrow's dreams, today's reality.

Open my eyes, dear Lord,
to see the gifts and graces
you have given
for this stage of my life.
And if I need to live more simply,
give more sacrificially,
step beyond my comfort zone
more courageously,
or simply love more devotedly,
help me to sing my heart's song
to the music you have written,
one note at a time.

The Past Is a Foreign Country

The past is a foreign country: they do things differently there.

L. P. HARTLEY

~

If becoming a grandmother was only a matter of choice,
I should advise every one of you straightaway to become one.
There's no fun for old people like it.

HANNAH WHITTAL SMITH

~

Being grandparents sufficiently removes us from the
responsibility of their upbringing, that we can be friends.

ALLAN FROME

~

We turn to Grandmother, trusting that she will help us
find answers, show us beauty and wonder, and call us to
full personhood. She not only knows what we do not know,
she is also wise enough to take time with us until we learn
it. No other woman can make a child feel so handsome,
so clever, so skilful, so loved, as a grandmother.

KRISTEN JOHNSON INGRAM

At last I've met him, Lord,
that precious grandson, born so far away.
Now no longer newly born,
with wobbly head and barely focused eyes,
but six months old,
and yet surprisingly
quite happy to be handed to a stranger,
surveying me as if to say,
"We meet at last."

As we gazed at one another,
blue eyes meeting brown,
my mind shot back,
then forward over three decades,
his mother's lifetime,
freeze-framed and full of memories.

Of course the way of "doing parenthood" today
is very different
from when our daughter was a child.
Somehow
motherhood did not require the expertise
in diet and in gadget maintenance
that it does now.

These days, a monitor alerts us
when he awakens,
and car seats, baby slings, and strollers
that really need an engineer to set them up
are every day necessities, it seems.

Where once a baby slept wrapped tight in blankets
to keep him warm,

he now lies on his back
and we must feel him often to make sure
he's not too hot.
Food that once was offered
without a thought of allergy or harm
is now regarded
as tantamount to poison.

But thankfully, dear Lord,
some things don't change.
Peekaboo is still a lovely game,
and ducks still swim expectant,
demanding bread with loud, impatient quacks,
their jewel-bright feathers glistening in the sun.

I thank you, Lord,
that buttercups still shine in sunny meadows,
reflecting on an upturned chin
to see if you like butter.
And stories that his mother used to love
have stood the test of time.

David and Goliath show that bullies
can be sent about their business,
while Noah can load up his ark
without a hint of interference
from departments of health and safety!

And best of all, dear Lord,
I do not need certification
of any kind to pray.
I can teach my grandchild
the simple words of childhood prayers,

explaining
that you are constantly as close to us as breathing,
nearer than hands and feet,
and that together
we can call upon your help
in every situation.

Prayers in the Night

He who dwells in the shelter of the Most High
will rest in the shadow of the Almighty.
I will say of the Lord, "He is my refuge and my fortress,
my God, in whom I trust" . . .
He will cover you with his feathers,
and under his wings you will find refuge . . .
You will not fear the terror of night . . .
nor the pestilence that stalks in the darkness . . .
For he will command his angels concerning you
to guard you in all your ways.

PSALM 91:1–11

~

Jesus, tender Shepherd, hear me;
Bless thy little Lamb tonight.
Through the darkness be thou near me;
Keep me safe till morning light.
Amen.

TRADITIONAL PRAYER

Dear Lord, I tumbled into bed so tired
I fell asleep
the moment that my head touched the pillow.
But now I am awake
and dawn is still some hours away.

I long to go to sleep once more,
but though I've tossed and turned,
rearranged the bedclothes,
closed the curtains,
opened the window,
and even sat downstairs to read a little,
sleep will not come.

On nights like these, dear Lord,
it's very hard
to keep the lions of worry from my mind.
For hard as I may try,
the problems I can push away while I am up and active—
concerns about my children, money,
decisions for the future—
come sneaking back,
a hundred times more
    terrifying,
when it is dark and still.

And then there is the
    house, Lord.
The creaks and clicks
    that I would never
    hear by day
sound loud and sinister at
    night.
And as the wind sighs
    through the trees
outside my bedroom
    window,
I wonder if I'll still live here next year.
Will I be able

I had feelings of fear about the future . . .
The devil kept on whispering, "It's all right
now, but what about afterwards? You are
going to be very lonely." . . . And I turned
to my God in a kind of desperation and
said, "Lord, what can I do? How can I go
on to the end?" And he said, "None of
them that trust in Me shall be desolate."
That word has been with me ever since.

AMY CARMICHAEL, ON "WEIGHING THE
COST" OF FULL-TIME MISSIONARY WORK

to afford the maintenance
if noises in the attic
signify some overlarge repair bill
and if the dripping bathroom tap
activates a flood
right through the kitchen ceiling?

Please help me, Lord.
For it's at times like these
I miss my husband more than ever.
But you have said
that I can rest within your everlasting arms.
Will you enable me to do just that?
And as I do,
please take away the tension
that is the root cause of my headache
and my twitching limbs.

I give you any discontent
about the path marked out for me,
and envy of the friends who seem to have
easier lives.
Please help me to resolve
that what is in my powers to do,
I'll tackle with your strength.
All the things that may lurk in the future,
about which in this present moment
I can do nothing,
I place into your loving hands
to keep
until the time when I must deal with them,
if that occurs.

Seize the Day

> *"Be dressed ready for service and keep your lamps burning,*
> *like men waiting for their master to return from a wedding*
> *banquet . . . You also must be ready, because the Son of Man*
> *will come at an hour when you do not expect him."*
>
> LUKE 12:35–40

~

> *I have one desire now—to live a life of reckless abandon for*
> *the Lord, putting all my energy and strength into it.*
>
> ELISABETH ELLIOT, THROUGH GATES OF SPLENDOR

~

> *Our care should not be to have lived*
> *long as to have lived enough.*
>
> SENECA

Dear Lord, I really can't believe that she is gone.
It seems incredible that somebody
whom I have known since early teens
and met with just a month ago,
to spend a day
talking about our lives from school days onward,
is really dead.

She seemed so full of life, Lord,
talking about the plans she had for worldwide travel,

the antics of her grandchildren,
and how these days she struggled
to reconcile
the simple faith we shared as teenagers
with practices within a more traditional church.

I don't think she had ceased to trust you, Lord,
but maybe she was following from afar.
For she confessed
that prayer and Bible reading
were no longer
an important part of her routine,
and that she disagreed with much of what was done
within the church worldwide.

I thank you, Lord,
that in our time together
you gave me opportunities to speak of you.
Indeed she asked a question about faith
before we'd settled down to drink our coffee,
and she returned to it so often in that day.
So I am trusting that she's now with you,
and I can leave her in your loving arms.
I pray that you will comfort
her stricken family,
so suddenly bereaved.

But Lord it's been a salutary lesson.
If you should call me home, as you did her,
would I be ready?
Would I have no unfinished business
with family or friends?

And would I know that I had lived my life,
making the most of every day
and taking every opportunity
to serve and please you?

Please help me, Lord.
Help me to keep such short accounts with you
and with the other people
that there would be no issues
that needed your forgiveness,
or words of love and thankfulness unspoken.

And please help me
to grasp and savor every good and perfect gift
so at the end of life,
however long or short that life might be,
it can be said of me,
"Here is God's beloved child.
She loved life and lived love."

All their life in this world and all their
adventures in Narnia had only been the
cover and the title page: now at last
they were beginning Chapter One of the
Great Story, which no one on earth has
read; which goes on forever; in which
every chapter is better than the one
before.

C. S. LEWIS

Downsizing

You will go out in joy and be led forth in peace;
the mountains and hills will burst into song before you,
and all the trees of the field will clap their hands.

ISAIAH 55:12

~

A wise woman builds her home,
but a foolish woman tears it down with her own hands.

PROVERBS 14:1 NLT

~

Lord, you have assigned me my portion and my cup;
you have made my lot secure.
The boundary lines have fallen for me in pleasant places;
surely I have a delightful inheritance.

PSALM 16:5–6

I'll mark this in my diary, Lord,
as a momentous day,
for after many months of arguments
and wrestling with reality,
decisions have been made,
and we have finally agreed that it is time to move.
"Downsizing" is what they call it, Lord.
A horrid word to me,

because it speaks of loss
and lack of space,
increasing age and lessening capacity.

And you know just how much of "us"
is wrapped up in this home,
where we have lived our lives
for more than forty years.
Each room,
which may have changed its designated use a dozen times,
has witnessed tears and laughter,
friends and family
gathering to celebrate or mourn,
and strangers finding welcome.

Lord, if we are now to find a smaller home,
what will I do with all the "things"
that we've collected through the years?
The childhood toys so lovingly restored
for grandchildren,
the books
and souvenirs from countries far away?

I know my kitchen cupboards
are full of pans that I no longer use;
sorting those will be a weeklong task.
And when I think about the attic
and rooms for guests,
which though used only rarely
are full of things
for which we had no other home,
I shudder

and wonder where I'll find the energy
to sort through boxes
and clean out the closets.

Thank you for the adult children
who've offered help,
and who will now perhaps
take their possessions back to their own homes.
Please give me joy in passing on
the things
for which we will no longer have the space.
Younger families
both need them
and will use them often.

Oh help us, Lord.
My husband is much less affected
by physical surroundings.
And he would probably move on
without a backward glance,
glad to be released from yard responsibilities
and keeping up the fabric of a home
that is beyond our needs.
"We'll have more freedom then," he tells me,
looking, as always, on the brighter side,
"and there will still be room for family and other guests,
but just not all at once!"

So be it, Lord.
Decisions have been made.
Please guide us to the home you have for us.
And as the serpent sheds its skin

to make growth possible,
help us to take the best of life "before"
and with it to create a new reality
that will fit perfectly
with all that you have planned for us
in this new season of our lives.

A Life Complete

"I have brought you glory on earth by completing the work you gave me to do."

JOHN 17:4

~

"My sword I give to him that shall succeed me in my pilgrimage, and my courage and skill to him that can get it. My marks and scars I carry with me, to be witness for me that I have fought His battles who will now be my rewarder" . . . *So [Mr. Valiant for Truth] passed over, and all the trumpets sounded for him on the other side.*

JOHN BUNYAN, PILGRIM'S PROGRESS

~

To touch the soul of another human being is to walk on holy ground.

STEPHEN R. COVEY

~

*That best portion of a good man's life,
His little, nameless, unremembered acts
Of kindness and of love.*

WILLIAM WORDSWORTH

There were so many funerals that summer, Lord.
Some, simple gatherings of aging friends;
others, almost state occasions—
the latter packed
with those who worked with the deceased,
and valued his contribution
to their profession.
They came with kind words of appreciation,
taking the front seats,
anxious both to see and be seen.

We often praise those with the obvious gifts, Lord.
Up-front and public profiles seem to be
the way to get things done,
give life significance,
leave lasting marks upon the world.
But on this day,
some five years after his death,
who remembers?
What makes a life have lasting impact
outside the loving circle
of family and friends?

It seems that it's not always the well known, Lord,
who leave enduring legacies,
but ordinary people
with relatively hidden lives,
who still have touched the lives of others
with words of counsel, words of love,
and words of faith and hope.
They pointed those they meet to you,
challenging them to give
their utmost for your highest purposes.

These people you have changed
will remember
the impact of your servant's life
and will themselves be true memorials,
investments that endure for all eternity,
earning for your faithful witnesses
the only accolade that really matters:
"Well done, good and faithful servant! . . .
Come and share your master's happiness."[14]

[Jesus] was born in an obscure village, the child of a peasant woman. He grew up in another village. He worked in a carpenter shop until He was thirty. Then for three years He was an itinerant preacher. He never owned a home. He never wrote a book. He never held an office. He never had a family. He never went to college. He never put His foot inside a big city. He never traveled two hundred miles from the place He was born. He never did one of the things that usually accompany greatness. He had no credentials but himself . . . While still a young man, the tide of popular opinion turned against him. His friends ran away. One of them denied him. He was turned over to his enemies. He went through the mockery of a trial. He was nailed upon a cross between two thieves. While he was dying his executioners gambled for the only piece of property he had on earth—his coat. When he was dead, he was laid in a borrowed grave through the pity of a friend.

Twenty long centuries have come and gone, and today he is a centerpiece of the human race and leader of the column of progress. I am far within the mark when I say that all the armies that ever marched, all the navies that were ever built, all the parliaments that ever sat, and all the kings that ever reigned, put together, have not affected the life of man upon this earth as powerfully as has that one solitary life.

DR. JAMES ALLAN FRANCIS, "ONE SOLITARY LIFE"

Notes

1. C. Austin Miles, "I Come to the Garden," 1912.

2. See Luke 10:25–37.

3. See John 1:39.

4. Quotation taken from *The Word for Today*, published by United Christian Broadcasters, Westport Road, Stoke on Trent ST6 4JF. Free copies of this devotional are available in the UK and Northern Ireland.

5. See Exodus 14, 1 Samuel 17, and Joshua 6.

6. To be "made redundant" is to be fired from employment.

7. Quotation taken from *The Word for Today*, published by United Christian Broadcasters, Westport Road, Stoke on Trent ST6 4JF.

8. Ephesians 4:15.

9. Quotation by John Oxenham.

10. Philippians 2:14 KJV.

11. Psalm 16:5–6.

12. See Matthew 2:11. Myrrh is an embalming ointment. It signifies both suffering and death, pointing to the fact that Jesus was born to die for the sins of the world. One of the burial spices mentioned in John 19:39 was myrrh.

13. See John 15:13.

14. Matthew 25:23.

Note to the Reader

The publisher invites you to share your response to the message of this book by writing Discovery House Publishers, P.O. Box 3566, Grand Rapids, MI 49501, U.S.A. For information about other Discovery House books, music, videos, or DVDs, contact us at the same address or call 1-800-653-8333. Find us on the Internet at http://www.dhp.org/ or send e-mail to books@dhp.org.

About the Author

*M*arion Stroud has been a bookworm since she memorized the rhyming couplets of the Rupert Bear stories when she was three years old. Marion always wanted to be a writer but trained initially to be a physical therapist. While studying at the Royal London Hospital in London's East End, she met her dental student husband-to-be. After they were married, Gordon set up his dental practice in Bedford, England, the town in which John Bunyan wrote *The Pilgrim's Progress*.

As soon as Marion "retired" from physiotherapy to have her first baby, she decided to fulfill two ambitions at once: to become a mother and a writer. She now has five adult children, seventeen grandchildren from ages eighteen months to nineteen years, and twenty-four published books to her name, many of which have been translated into up to fourteen different languages.

Living in Malaysia as a child gave Marion a heart for people from different nations. She works with Media Associates International to mentor and encourage writers in countries where little Christian literature is written or published.

Marion and her husband love entertaining, walking, reading, and traveling. They are active in the church they helped to found more than thirty years ago. They also lead a small group where they offer pastoral support, and together learn more about living out their faith in daily life.